SKI FITNESS

OLLIE MARTIN

Second Edition

Editorial & Design Services: The Write Factor
www.thewritefactor.co.uk

Thank You

To my beautiful wife Julia and children Lily and Alice,
who have taught me lots and have put up with me –
and not forgetting my faithful training partner, Bruce.

To the many people and organisations I have had the pleasure of learning from including, University of Northumbria, CHEK Institute, American College of Sports Medicine, Exuberant Animal, Matthew Wallden of Primal Lifestyle, Judy Lorraine of the Master Ding Academy, Ski Club of Great Britain and my clients.

To professional skier, Bethany Widdup, my fantastic model for the book and website. I'm grateful to her for the long journeys she made for the photoshoots and her patience and enthusiasm for the project. I wish her every luck in her career.

To Lorna and her team at The Write Factor for their amazing design of the book.

For Lily and Alice

About the author

Ollie Martin is a holistic health and high performance author, presenter and coach. He has a BSc (Hons.) Sport Science, is a CHEK Practitioner and has 20 years of experience coaching athletes. He played semi-professional rugby union, is a Ski Club GB 'Gold' skier and spends much of his time 'playing' in the Alps. He is also author of Uncommon Sense: A Practical Guide to Health, Weight Loss & Vitality and runs a health and performance consultancy based in Surrey, UK.

www.olliemartin.com
www.skifitness.tv

CONTENTS

Chapter 1: Introduction

Chapter 2: The Programme

Chapter 3: Performance Exercises

Chapter 4: Success Information

GLOSSARY

BB .... Barbell

BOSU .... Acronym for 'Both Sides Up' an inflatable dome shaped balance challenge aid.

BW .... Bodyweight i.e. no extra weights

DB .... Dumbbell

Isometric................. Strength work without any movement

MB .... Medicine Ball

Plyos .... Plyometrics (rebounding movements like jumping)

Prone .... Face/front downwards

Reps .... Repetitions of each exercise

RM .... Repetition Maximum (the maximum weight you can lift, eg. 1RM is the maximum lift you can lift once)

RR .... Repetition reserve - a number of repetitions you could complete but you do not complete to ensure optimum technique.

SB .... Stability Ball (also means Swiss Ball)

Secs .... Seconds

Sets .... A number of repetitions is a set

Supine .... Face/front upwards

Tech. .... Focus on precise technique rather than number or difficulty

Tempo .... Speed of exercise in seconds, with an option to split into parts eg. 1-2-1 (see Chapter 4)

↘ .... The green shading linking exercises and arrow in rest section is a 'Superset' which means you go straight on to the linked exercise without rest and then, if completing another set, rest the stated time, and then go back to the first exercise (like a mini-circuit)

TRX .... Brand name for a suspension strap, often used for pulling exercises.

CHAPTER 1

INTRODUCTION

I wrote this book because I do not believe stationary cycling and Pilates will benefit your skiing as much as you hope it will. As far as I'm aware, performed correctly, skiing is neither akin to sitting or lying down, and don't even get me started on a squat with a ball behind your back!

Fitness is very specific - you get what you train for. The winner of the Tour de France may be the fittest man on the planet, but he could not win the London Marathon and probably could not even ski down the Hahnenkamm, let alone win it.

I am passionate about skiing and believe that a bit of smart training beforehand can dramatically improve your 'ski fun.' I have put together a comprehensive ski-specific training programme that you can follow easily whatever your level. Furthermore, the detailed instructions, progressions and enhancements will enable you to tailor your training to your individual needs.

I have fine-tuned this over 20 years of training top athletes, obese couch-potatoes, children, septuagenarians and all those in-between. Yes, there might be some good 'ski-specific' exercises left out of the programme, but trying to do them all creates a poor programme. Rather than lots of exercises that try to replicate the key skiing movements, I have put together a systematically planned (periodised) conditioning programme. A periodised conditioning programme takes you much further than just trying to get fit doing ski-specific circuits; better still, it gets you much fitter for skiing than ... just skiing. This is because it identifies weaknesses in your chain of movements and strengthens them. The programme starts by building a core base, strengthening key muscles, improving power and only then moving on to the ski-specific endurance exercises you probably know.

CHAPTER 1

Myth: The best way of getting fit for skiing is to ski – WRONG

The best way to get fit for any activity is firstly, to become a fitter, stronger, better aligned 'human athlete' and secondly, to tailor your training specifically for your activity/sport. After the activity you then need to counter the biases inherent in the sport with some specific rehabilitation exercises. Luckily skiing has few biases and is very complementary to the human athlete unlike the rounded-back body position in a sport like cycling, for example, but you will still need some rehabilitation after skiing.

The programme includes:

- A differing start and end point for different ski aspirations and fitness levels
- Periodisations
- Detailed schedules
- Pictures and detailed descriptions
- Why you do each exercise (I rarely see this detailed in other programmes but is the key to success – if you do not know what an exercise is trying to achieve, how do you know its importance or if you're doing it correctly?)
- Videos online at www.skifitness.tv

THE HOLY TRINITY OF SKI PERFORMANCE

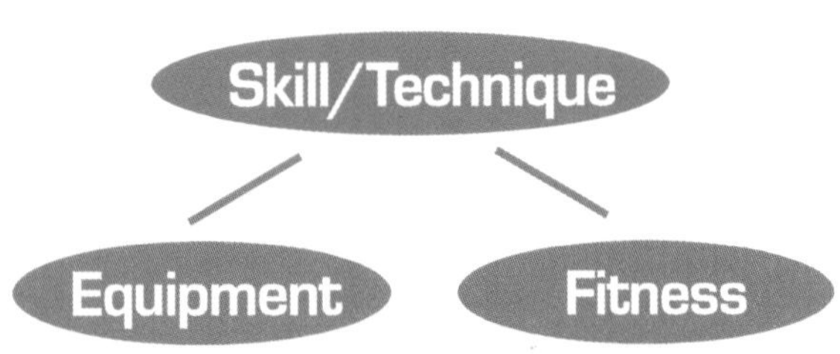

These three elements are totally interlinked and are key to maximising the fun of your ski holiday. If any of these are out of balance it can have drastic effects and can be dangerous. For example, for years I have chosen a ski trip based on the ski standard of the group i.e., we are all the same standard skiers (a fantastic concept from The Ski Club of Great Britain). I spend three to five months training (as per this book) and generally feel one of the fittest in the group. This enables me to ski to the full extent of my skill level all day every day for a week – even that long pitch of deep powder at the end of the day!

However, one year I decided to change my boots and got it slightly wrong. Firstly, I did not have enough time to 'break-in' the new boots and so this caused foot pain. Secondly, the new boots did not fit my skis in the same way as the old ones and should have had a slightly different setting. As the group was of a high standard, the first morning we went straight into a steep couloir (narrow gully) with deepish powder. I know 'a bad workman blames his tools' but my skis fell off on the first difficult pitch, slicing my knee open, with me ending up in the medi-centre centre needing 13 stitches. I was under strict medical instructions not to fall during the next few days and this entailed a change of technique, making me sit back, which wasted energy. Furthermore, I had not worked out that the bindings were not tight enough for the new skis yet and so found myself falling over in deep powder more than I should have. As I'm sure you know, falling over then finding and putting your skis back on is one of the most tiring things ever!

So, I was fantastically fit and in the right skill level for the group but, equipment problems were 'haemorrhaging' my fitness. I was getting very tired and started to become a danger to myself and to the group as I was almost not able to keep up: a situation I do not want to repeat again!

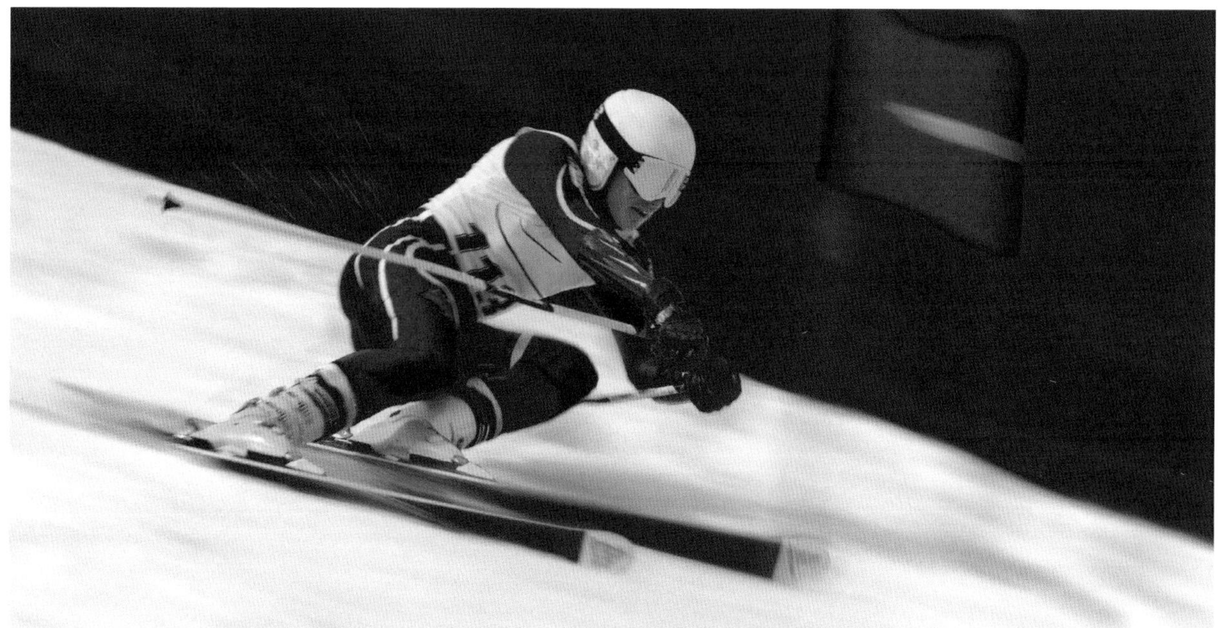

Similarly, if your skill level is the lowest in the group, you will use more energy than anyone else. I'm sure most of us have experienced both sides of the equation: waiting for someone to catch up whilst having a lovely rest and then skiing straight off when they arrive, giving them no time to regain their energy.

I believe it is absolutely crucial to be in the top half of fitness in the group. This book will make sure you are!

THE 3 SECRETS TO SKI FITNESS SUCCESS

No. 1 Strength, Power, Endurance

- Downhill skiing is mostly a power/endurance sport
- Lack of muscle strength and stability haemorrhages aerobic energy
- There is very little benefit to stationary cycling for ski fitness
- Fitness is very specific, i.e the Tour de France winner could not win the London marathon
- Core strength is more important than aerobic exercise
- You get little or no strength benefit from aerobic exercise but you do get aerobic benefit from resistance exercise

No. 2 Fun, Fun, Fun

- If it hurts you're doing it incorrectly
- Be creative – change every session, just a little, by playing with the exercises
- Periodisation (see below)

No. 3 Learn and Personalise

- You are unique and so should your programme be
- Make sure you review Chapter 4 at the end of this book – it will help you understand more deeply
- Listen to your body, understand it and develop your own programme with the knowledge herein
- Learn from the 'pain teacher'

CHAPTER 1

THE PERIODISED PROGRAMME

The main reason for writing this programme and the key to your success is the concept of periodisation. This basically means starting at the correct level for you and steadily progressing in complexity, hardness (intensity) and ski- specificity. Most skiers start their ski-specific training somewhere in the middle in terms of complexity and hardness. They then complete the same programme week after week for the whole ski training period and they do this year after year!

However, I'm sorry to say there aren't any ski-specific exercises and there is certainly not one ski-specific programme. Instead, by following this programme, we endeavour to condition the body to be fitter, stronger, more aligned, injury-proof and powerful in order to deal with the many and varied rigours a ski holiday throws at the body. We do this by undertaking a number of different phases of exercise for a period of time – say four to six weeks – each with differing objectives but, generally progressing in terms of hardness and complexity. This is periodisation.

This programme has the following periodised phases:

Phase 1 – Fun
Phase 2 – Core Rehabilitation
Phase 3 – Functional Strength
Phase 4 – Power & Single Leg Strength
Phase 5 – Power Endurance Circuits
Phase 6 – Advanced Power/Endurance Plyometrics

The duration of this programme, followed closely, is three to five months, depending on initial fitness and desired level.

Note: You do not always progress in a linear fashion: it is normally a case of three steps forward, one step back to ensure no ligament or tendon is left behind and that you are not over-training. In this programme, we have sample schedules and recovery circuits to help you achieve this.

"Periodisation is all about maximising the results of training. By effectively varying the timing and intensity of workouts, athletes will achieve the greatest gains in strength, speed, power and endurance."
– Tudor Bompa, Olympic Coach & Periodisation Expert

EXERCISE DESCRIPTIONS – THE WHY

Incorporated in your detailed exercise description chapter is 'why' I have selected this particular exercise for you to perform. In most programmes or books I see, exercises are given with no explanation as to what they are meant to do for you or why they are good for you. Sometimes it is obvious, but not always. If you know which muscles you are using, you will get better results through 'cognitive activation' (the mind activating the correct muscles). You will also know if you are doing the exercise incorrectly because you will not feel the muscle working. I also try and explain why each exercise is good for your skiing – this 'big picture' always helps with motivation and so improves the exercise performance.

THE HOW

Precise technique is very important when undertaking an exercise programme. 'The How' paragraph in the Chapter Three includes detailed descriptions of how to complete each exercise. It is important to follow these as closely as possible to ensure the correct technique and therefore achieve the proper effect. It is useful to reread these once you have competed the exercise/ phase a few times to help fine tune your technique. These are supplemented by the video tutorials on www.skifitness.tv

PROGRESSIONS

This paragraph on many of the exercise descriptions enables you to make the exercise harder once you have mastered the correct technique of the initial exercise. This tailoring of each exercise to your own progression speed ensures consistent challenge and better results.

OUTDOOR/HOME ALTERNATIVE

Gym not necessary!

Outdoor exercise is always better than indoor exercise.

Although this might look like a gym-based conditioning programme, most of the exercises can be performed at home or even better, outside. Sometimes a little imagination is needed, but in many circumstances, I have given an 'outdoor alternative'.

The benefits of outdoor training include:

- more stimulus, so perception of hardness and duration is reduced
- there are many health benefits of being out in nature, but if nothing else, you will recover more quickly
- daylight enhances your circadian rhythm (sleep/ wake cycle) i.e. better sleep and quicker recovery
- varied terrain and training apparatus (trees, logs, rocks, hills, uneven ground, play equipment) means the muscles/joints will be stronger in more situations and so increases performance, reduces risk of injury and yes, quicker recovery times
- more realistic for skiing by training in the elements: wind, rain, sun – sometimes it is slippery, sometimes dry, sometimes cold, sometimes hot – helps acclimatise the body
- fresh air enhances breathing, health and recovery times
- more space to complete some of the exercises
- exercises can be more dynamic, when appropriate, outdoors
- vitamin D, the sunshine vitamin, helps prevent disease

Useful equipment:

- stability ball
- resistance band
- something for pull-ups (rope around fixed point, rings etc.)
- wobble board (alternative for BOSU)

'You need an average of at least 10-15 minutes of sunlight every day to prevent cancer.'
From, Over a Million People Die Every Year From Lack of Sun Exposure by Dr Mercola

CHAPTER 1

SKI FITNESS MYTHS TRUE OR FALSE?

Myth: Aerobic/cardio-vascular (CV) training is best

False: If you were only going to do one type of training, strength training would be best. Downhill skiing is mostly a power/endurance sport and lack of muscle strength and stability haemorrhages aerobic energy.

Myth: Pilates is good for ski fitness

False: Pilates is a fantastic system designed for professional dancers to rehabilitate their back by working the muscles without the 'axial load' (spinal pressure from gravity) of dancing. Pilates is rehabilitation and is only useful if you need early stage rehabilitation for your back. Many people do need this, but make the mistake of not progressing their training back to 'normal' standard. They then compound this further, by not further progressing with the addition of axial load to the high performance needed for sliding down a steep, slippery mountain.

Myth: Squats with a ball behind your back are good for fitness

False: Again these are rehabilitation exercises, and are only useful if you cannot function or squat to 'normal' human being standard (see Chapter 4, Progression Exercises). Progression is the key.

Myth: Stationary cycling is good for skiing because it works the thigh muscles

False: Stationary cycling does work the thigh muscles, but not in the way these muscles are used for skiing. In reality, stationary cycling actually makes the thigh muscles relatively weaker for skiing because they have been worked to become relatively stronger in the sitting down, cycling position. This type of exercise does not strengthen the core, it does not address knee alignment or balance, and is generally not performed at the right angle to aid skiing.

Myth: Ski Circuit classes are good for skiing fitness

False: You cannot ever exactly replicate a day or week's skiing in a class format. Ski fitness classes tend to work endurance not strength. A class format is not tailored to your unique needs and so it will also exacerbate the weak links in your 'movement chain'.

Myth: Skiing is the best, if not the only, way to get fit for a ski holiday

False: When skiing you will actually get progressively weaker and more susceptible to injury because you won't have enough rest. It also exacerbates weak links in your movement chain and will do this increasingly the

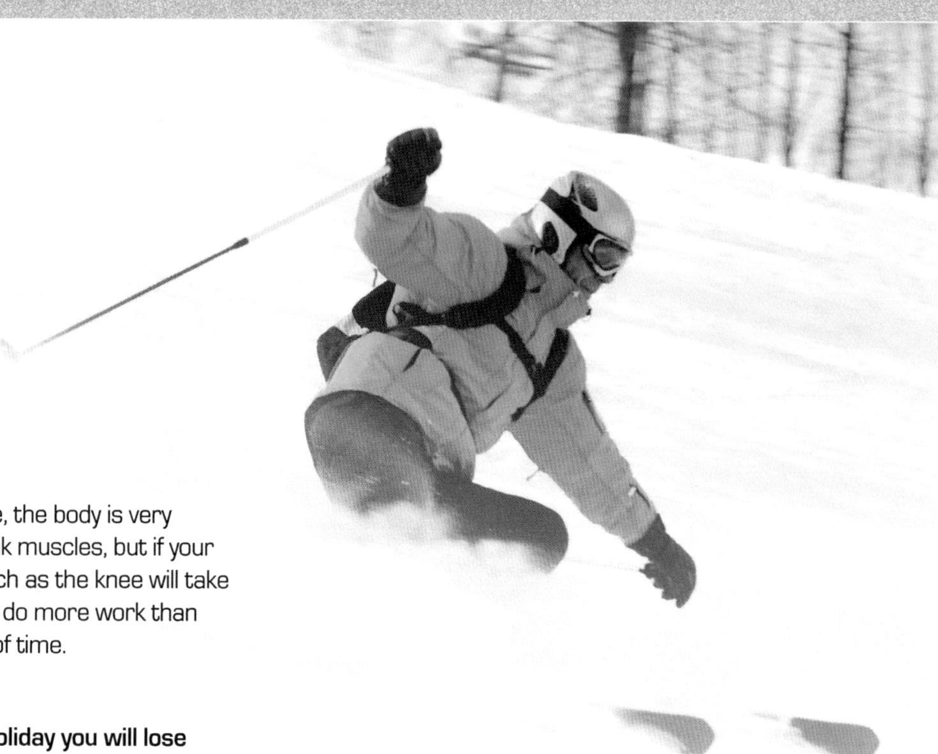

more tired you get. For example, the body is very clever and will work around weak muscles, but if your core is relatively weak, joints such as the knee will take more of the strain. When joints do more work than muscles injury is only a matter of time.

Myth: If you eat less on a ski holiday you will lose weight

False: You might lose weight but, you will not lose body fat. If you reduce calories you will have less energy available for skiing and your body will start to store energy as fat, 'for emergency use only'. You will also burn and use up muscle, and dehydrate – which accounts for any temporary weight loss but, you will have more body fat and less energy to do anything about it!

Myth: Skiing is one of the best activities for health

True: Skiing is fun, gets you out into the fresh air and is a very functional exercise with only a few biases to human alignment, i.e. it is in line with the way the body has been designed to move through its 4 million years of evolution.

Myth: You don't need strong feet for skiing as they are supported by hard boots.

False: Surprisingly, your feet work very hard when you are skiing. Weak feet are the main cause of boot pain. Strengthen your feet and lower legs by training barefoot or using running shoes with minimal support.

Myth: Don't eat yellow snow

True: Always good advice!

THE PROGRAMME

HOW TO USE THE PROGRAMME

There are six phases of the programme, carefully designed to progress a complete beginner or the fittest athlete. By going through the phases in order you create a strong base, ensuring a high peak!

Which phases you do and in which order is determined by two variables:

1 your ski aspirations
2 your self assessment results

Each phase has a sample schedule which shows you optimal frequency and rest days between each session. However, it is only a guideline and can be tailored to your other time commitments and how quickly (or slowly) you recover. In the schedule there is a timescale in weeks showing how long you should do each training phase for before you move on. If in doubt, complete the greater number of weeks i.e. Phase 2 gives a 2-4 week timescale so complete 4 weeks.

Phase 1 – Fun (all year)

This is for everyone all the time. If you are not moving your body every day already this is where you need to start. But it is also useful for the off-season (summer) to keep you in good condition. It is what exercise or 'movement' is all about – finding something you enjoy and doing it regularly.

Phase 2 – Core Rehabilitation (2-4 weeks)

A high peak needs a solid 'base'. Your 'core', simply your tummy, back and bottom, are the 'base' that all body movements come from. Before you strengthen any part of your body you want to coordinate (activate key muscles) and then strengthen your core. You cannot be a ski athlete without a strong and stable core platform.

PS yes, if you're a skier, you're an athlete!

Phase 3 – Functional Strength (6 – 8 Weeks)

Rather than the 'old school' notion of training individual muscles and body parts, functional strength trains the body in movement patterns which are 'functional' to everyday life and most sporting movements. Functional training always uses the core, combining the upper and lower body and is generally performed standing up, like life and skiing.

Phase 4 – Power & Single Leg Strength (4 Weeks)

Once you have achieved functional strength, you can then convert this strength into power. Power is a combination of speed and strength and is very important for skiing. For advanced athletes, Phase 4 introduces power and single leg strength, creating forces similar to dynamic skiing.

Phase 5 – Power Endurance Circuits (4 weeks)

For intermediate athletes, we recommend converting functional strength to power endurance in the form of ski-specific circuits. Power is speed and strength and endurance is being able to keep up intervals over a longer period of time. This most closely replicates the forces in skiing.

Phase 6 – Advanced Power/Endurance Plyometrics (4 weeks)

Our extreme athletes finish their training with high intensity plyometrics. Building on all the previous phases, this is dynamic jump training, using the recoil of muscles fibres to explosively change direction, over and over again. This is only for injury free athletes with optimal body alignment, strong and stable joints and a strong core. A minimum of four rest days are needed between plyometric sessions (more information in Chapter 4).

WARM-UP AND COOL DOWNS

Page 28-29 gives you stretches and mobilisations to help you warm-up before each session and cool down after each session.

STRETCHING PROGRAMME

See page 24. Runs concurrently with all phases.

RECOVERY PROGRAMME

Chapter 4 explains about the training effect and the need to recover optimally (supercompensation). The recovery programme speeds up recovery and, in doing so, builds health. It does this through non-stressful, slow movement and breathing techniques that assist the heart in pumping blood and oxygen around the body. You can do the recovery programme everyday and at any time. It works well in the evening as it reduces stress hormones and increases sleep hormones.

TAPER

A one to two week reduction in training volume/ intensity to ensure you have fully recovered from your training before you go skiing (See Chapter 4).

SKI ASPIRATIONS

Choosing which standard/colour of ski runs you plan to ski will decide which programme/phases you should undertake. If you mainly ski on green and blue runs, phases 1 to 3 will be ideal. These require around two months preparation.

For skiers who want to ski the whole resort – green, blue, red and black runs - complete phase 1 to 5 but with the option to omit phase 4. This requires in the region of four to five months preparation.

For expert skiers who want to ski the whole mountain including itineraries, backcountry, guided and heli-skiing, complete phases 1 to 6, with option to omit Phase 5. This requires in the region of four to five months preparation.

SELF-ASSESSMENT

There are three assessments for you to complete:

SA1: Overhead squat
SA2: Lower abdominal core stability test
SA3: Measure around your middle at tummy button height

SCORING

If you score 'Poor' on all three tests, I would recommend seeing a fitness professional, ideally a CHEK Practitioner (see www.chekconect.com).

If you score 'Poor' or 'Moderate' in one or more of the tests, spend more time on Phases 1 to 3 as this will rehabilitate you to the required 'Good' standard in all three tests necessary for progressing on to Phase 4 and beyond.

If you scored 'Good' in all three tests, start the main programme at Phase 3 missing out Phase 2.

SA1: OVERHEAD SQUAT

Incorrect: knees rotating inwards

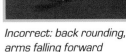

Incorrect: back rounding, arms falling forward

Stand with your feet shoulder-width apart and hold a broomstick (or something heavier) over your head with straight arms. Then perform 10 squats/sit-downs.

Self-assessment

Choose which of these three statements best describes your squat:

Good – No pain anywhere, arms stay straight, arms do not fall forward, hips stay straight, knees bend more than 90 degrees, knees stay in line with feet, feet do not rotate outwards, heels stay flat on floor.
Moderate – A twinge or two, arms come forward and bend a little, knees want to rotate inwards and feet want to rotate out but can be controlled, knees bend to 90 degrees, heels come up.
Poor – Pain anywhere, bent arms falling forward, restricted movement (hips not to 90 degrees), no control of knee tracking in line with feet.

SA2: LOWER ABDOMINAL CORE

This test is designed to see if you have the core coordination and control to choose what position to put your body in. A 'force' will come from an extremity – legs or arms – into your core. The response from your core will then decide the best position for the extremities to deal with the next force. If you have no core control, your spine will move in time with your extremities and will not be able to choose the best position, for example, keeping your knees in line with your feet. This will lead to reduced efficiency (fitness), poor performance and injury. But, do not panic! This test is also a progressive exercise in the programme so you can perfect it.

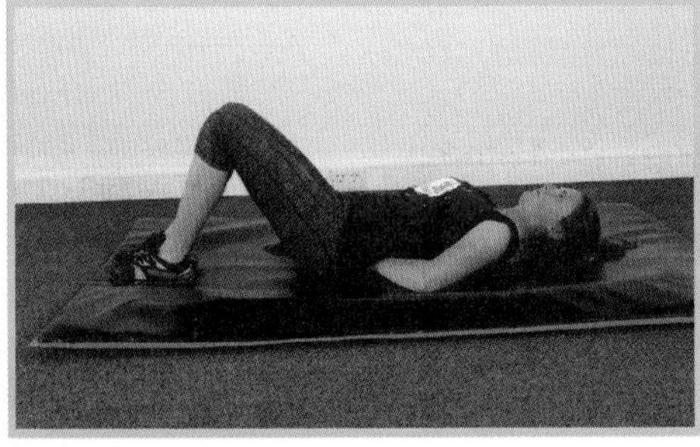

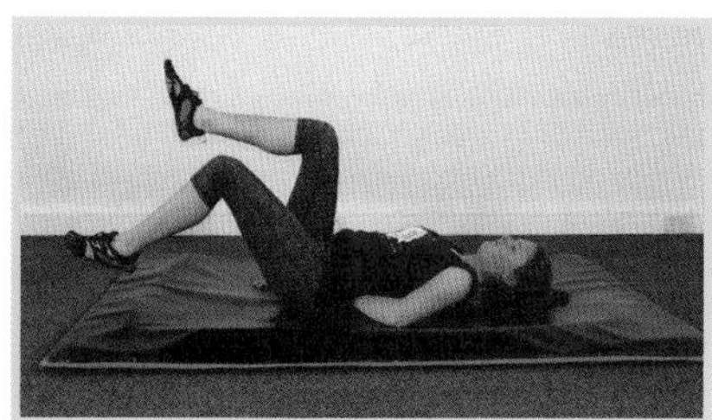
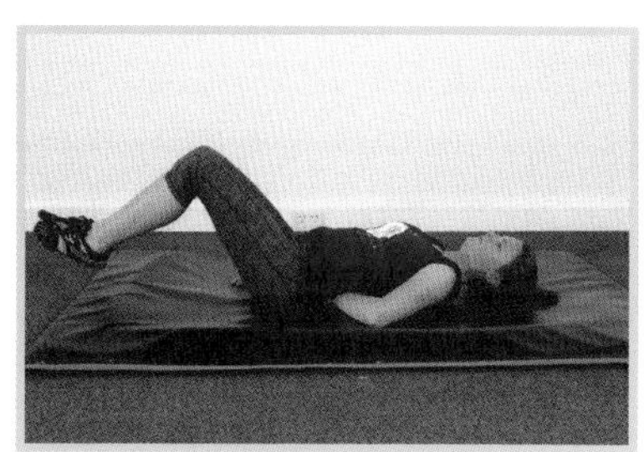

Lie with your back on the floor. Place the widest part of one hand facing down, in the small of your back directly behind your tummy button. Bring both legs up off the floor with knees at right angles. Draw your tummy button down by about one third (navel towards spine) and flatten back into your hand with about 50% pressure. Move legs, keeping 90-degree angle at the knees, towards the floor maintaining a constant 50% pressure on your hand.

Self-assessment

Choose which of these three statements best describes your movement:

Good – Constant 50% pressure on the hand, tummy draw-down maintained while two legs go down to floor, able to lightly touch and come back up again.
Moderate – Not possible with two legs, but possible with one leg.
Poor – Not possible to keep any constant pressure on the hand when legs move.

For more accuracy than just 'feeling' the pressure on your hand, you can use a pressure-cuff (such as those used for measuring blood pressure – a sphygmomanometer). Use the pressure-cuff instead of your hand, pumping it to 40-bar of pressure and then add another 30-bar by pressing your lower back down into the cuff for the exercise.

SA3: MEASURE AROUND YOUR MIDDLE AT TUMMY BUTTON HEIGHT

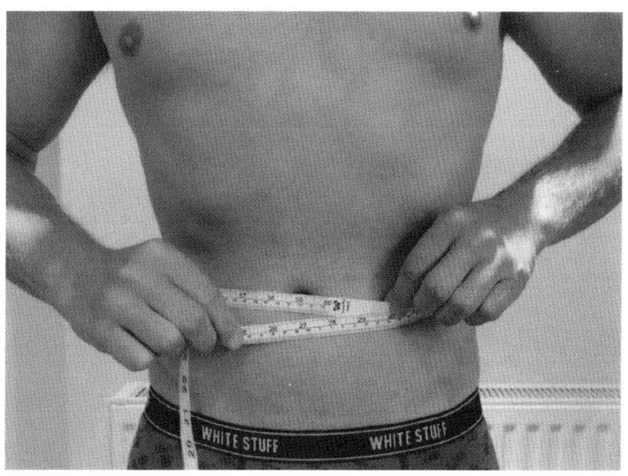

Self-assessment

Choose which of these three statements best describes your measurement:

Good – under 85cm
Moderate – under 100cm
Poor – over 100cm

CHAPTER 2

PHASE 1 : FUN

> ***'Become an exercise opportunist!'***

Timescale: all year

"See the world as your gym."

With busy lifestyles it is really important to become an 'exercise opportunist' – someone who takes every opportunity to exercise. 20 years of experience in fitness coaching has taught me that the people who are 'fit' are the ones that embed activity into their lifestyles. The really successful ones see the world as their gym. It is not all about intensive or hard-hitting fitness sessions when you are on a fitness drive; it is about lots of little bouts of movement throughout the day and the week. If you work behind a desk, you need to think about taking regular 'movement snacks', such as walking for five minutes every hour. This might not seem like much exercise, but in this case, 'the sum is greater than the parts' as regular movement helps the heart pump blood around the body (which is essential for health and therefore fitness), so it sure beats a cardio machine in the gym. Movement every hour is much better for the body than being physically inactive for days at a time then expending a massive burst of energy in the gym for 2 hours followed by inertia again for the rest of the week, month or even year!

Walking, hiking, barefoot running, mountain-biking, 'It' or 'Tag' with kids or dog, slacklining, adventure races/obstacle courses, gardening, ballroom dancing ...

As a human athlete you need daily fun and vigorous movement.

Movement Snacks:

- little and often
- variety in movement
- fit into lifestyle/work day
- sum is greater than the parts
- play/fun

FUN THEORY

If it's boring don't do it, even if you think it is good for you! If it is fun it will be good for you and you'll keep doing it. If it's boring, you could actually be retarding your movement patterns. For example spending too much time working your core on your back, (e.g. Pilates, or working your legs and heart too hard for too long without the need for skill or balance such as spinning) will actually 'retard' your movement patterns.

Fitness is very specific – if you train too long in one movement pattern you will become relatively weaker in other movement patterns.

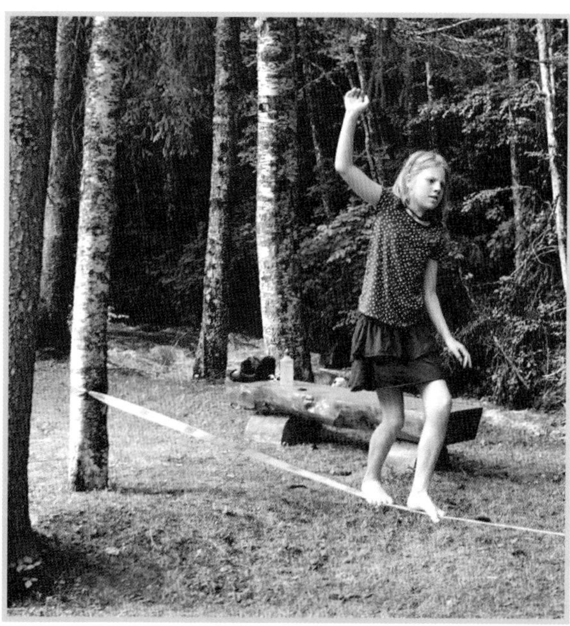

PHASE 2 : CORE REHABILITATION

Timescale: 2-4 weeks

PHASE 2 SESSION 1 (P2S1)

Exercise	Sets	Reps/Time	Intensity	Rest
Single Leg Shin/Toe Touches (Page 32)	1	8 each side	Bodyweight (BW)	-
Lower Abdominal 1-4 (Page 34)	4-10	10-20 secs	Tech.	20 sec
Ball Rollouts (Page 33)	4-10	10 secs	Tech.	20 sec

PHASE 2 SESSION 2 (P2S2)

Exercise	Sets	Reps / Time	Intensity	Rest
Squats (Page 36)	1-2	10-12	BW	1:00 minute
Lateral Lunges (Page 37)	1-2	16-20	BW	1:00
Ball Plank (Page 38)	1-4	10-20 secs	BW	0:20
SB Supine Offsets (Page 39)	1-2	10	BW	1:00
SB Wall Press (Page 40)	1-2	10-12	BW	1:00

PHASE 2 SAMPLE SCHEDULE

Week	Mon	Tues	Wed	Thurs	Fri	Sat	Sun
1	P2S1		P2S1		P2S1		
2	P2S1		P2S1		P2S1		P2S1
3	P2S2	P2S1		P2S1	P2S2		
4	P2S1	P2S2		P2S1	P2S2		

PHASE 3 : FUNCTIONAL STRENGTH

Timescale: 4-8 weeks

PHASE 3 SESSION 1 (P3S1)

Exercise	Sets	Reps / Time	Intensity	Rest	Tempo
Front Squat (Page 41)	2-4	8-10	2RR	2:00	212
Pull-up/ Body Row (Page 42)	1-3	8-10	1RR	1:00	112
Cable Press (Page 43)	1-3	8-10	2RR	1:00	112
Chek Shoulder Press (Page 44)	1-3	8-10	2RR	1:00	2322
Russian Twist (Page 45)	1-3	8-10	1RR	1:00	Fluid
LA4 (Page 34)	4-6	10-20secs	Tech.	0:20	Controlled

RR... Repetition Reserve - a number of repetitions you could complete but you do not complete to ensure optimum technique (see p97).

Tempo... speed in seconds of distinct movements in the exercise (see p97)

PHASE 3 SESSION 2 (P3S2)

Exercise	Sets	Reps / Time	Intensity	Rest	Tempo
Deadlift (Page 47)	2-4	8-10	2RR	2:00	212
Multi-d Lunges (Page 48)	1-3	20	1RR	1:00	112
MB Reverse Woodchop (Page 49)	1-3	8-10	2RR	1:00	112
Cable Pull (Page 50)	1-3	8-10	2RR	↘	2322
Ball Press-ups (Wall) (Page 51)	1-3	8-10	1RR	1:00	Fluid
SB Supine Offset Leg-lift (Page 52)	1-2	10	BW	1:00	333
Prone Feet Ball Roll (Page 53)	1-2	20	BW	1:00	Fluid

SAMPLE SCHEDULE

Week	Mon	Tues	Wed	Thurs	Fri	Sat	Sun
1	P3S1		P3S1		P3S1		
2	P3S1		P3S1		P3S1		
3	P3S1		P3S1		P3S1		
4	P3S2		P3S2		P3S2		
5	P3S1	P3S2		P3S1		P3S2	
6	P3S1	P3S2		P3S1		P3S2	
7	P3S1	P3S2		P3S1		P3S2	
8	P3S1	P3S2		P3S1		P3S2	

PHASE 4 : POWER AND SINGLE LEG STRENGTH

Timescale: Approx. 4 weeks (advanced only)

PHASE 4 SESSION 1 (P4S1)

Exercise	Sets	Reps / Time	Intensity	Rest	Tempo
BB Clean and Press (Rock Press) (Page 54)	3-5	8-10	1RR	3:00	Fast
Cable Jump Twist (Page 56)	3	30	High	↘	Fast
Single Leg Squats (Bench) (Page 56)	3	8-10	1RR	2:00	Controlled
Body Row (Pull-ups) (Page 58)	2-3	10-15	High	↘	Fast
Hands-on SB Press-ups (Feet on Swiss Ball) (Page 59)	2-3	8-10	High	1:00	Fast
SB Lower Abs Dynamic (Page 60)	2-3	10	High	↘	Fast
SB MB Power Sit-ups (Page 61)	2-3	10	High	1:00	Fast

Green shading indicates these two exercises should be completed in a 'superset' or mini-circuit i.e. complete one set of the first exercise then go straight onto next exercise, then rest, then complete next set of the first exercise and so on.

PHASE 4 SESSION 2 (P4S2)

Exercise	Sets	Reps / Time	Intensity	Rest	Tempo
Single Arm DB Snatch (Single Leg) (Page 62)	3-5	8-10	1RR	3:00	Fast
Cable Single Leg, Single Press (Page 63)	3	8-10	High	↘	Fast
Cable Single Leg Squat and Single Arm-pull (Page 63)	2-3	8-10	High	1:00	Fast
MB Washing Machine (Page 64)	2-3	30-60	High	↘	Fast
Lateral Dynamic Lunges with MB Loops (Page 65)	2-3	30-60	High	1:00	Fast
Kneeling/Standing on Swiss Ball (Page 66)					Fun

PHASE 4 SAMPLE SCHEDULE

Week	Mon	Tues	Wed	Thurs	Fri	Sat	Sun
1	P4S1		P4S1		P4S2		
2	P4S1		P4S2		P4S1		P4S2
3		P4S1	P4S2			P4S1	P4S2
4			P4S1		P4S2		

PHASE 5 POWER ENDURANCE CIRCUITS

(Advanced athletes might want to skip Phase 5.)

Timescale: Approx. 4 weeks

No rest between circuit exercises. Rest 4 minutes at end of circuit and repeat 3 to 5 times.

Moderate: Start off 30 secs each, then try 45 secs and 60 secs
Hard: Start off 60 secs each, then try 90 secs and 120s secs

PHASE 5 CIRCUIT 1 (P5C1)

BOSU Jumps/Circuit (Page 67)
Lateral Hops/Skaters (BOSU) (Page 68)
DB Get-ups (Page 69)
Skiing Jackknifes (Page 70)
SB Leg Curls (Page 70)
Russian Twists (Page 71)
Bench Lower Abs (Page 71)
Single Leg BOSU balance (Page 72)

PHASE 5 CIRCUIT 2 (P5C2)

Skipping (Page 73)
SB Prone Lateral Roll – feet on ball (Page 73)
SB Supine Bridge Leg Lifts (Page 74)
Lateral Lunge MB Loop-the-Loop (Page 74)
SB Prone Lateral Ball Rolls – arms on ball (Page 75)
SB Press-up and Jackknife (Page 76)
BOSU Squat Isometric Hold (Page 76)

PHASE 5 SAMPLE SCHEDULE

(Advanced athletes may want to skip Phase 5)

Week	Mon	Tues	Wed	Thurs	Fri	Sat	Sun
1	P5C1		P5C1		P5C1		
2	P5C2		P5C2		P5C2		
3	P5C1	P5C2		P5C1	P5C2		
4	P5C1	P5C2		P5C1	P5C2		P5C1

PHASE 6 ADVANCED POWER/ ENDURANCE PLYOMETRICS

Timescale: Approx. 4 weeks

PHASE 6 SESSION 1 (P6S1): PLYOMETRIC SESSION

Plyometric exercises (also known as 'jump-training') exert maximum force in short intervals of time with the goal of increasing power and strength. See Chapter 4 for more details.

(4-day recovery time)

1. Box Jumps (Page 77)
Standard/mixed/jump tyres
60 secs each set
3 minutes rest between sets
4 sets
4 mins rest before next exercise

2. Lateral Jumps Two-Footed (Page 78)
30 secs each set
90 secs rest between sets
4 sets
4 mins rest before next exercise

3. One-Footed Jumps (Page 79)
30-60 secs each set
3 minutes rest between sets
4 sets

Use the timings above as a starting point then vary them.

When you are doing these exercises and are choosing your intensity and timings think about when you are actually skiing. This is the ski-specific phase and we want you to replicate your own skiing as much as possible. For example, think about how you feel after a two hour hike, when you then have to produce near perfect 180 degree jump turns with tired legs in a narrow couloir. Then schedule your training i.e. time jumping and rest time according to how long you would ski a pitch for and how long you would rest for. Play around with different timings to replicate real skiing and its differing rest periods.

PHASE 6 SESSION 2 (P6S2): DYNAMIC STRENGTH (CREATIVE FUN)

This is a play session – mix it up, use what equipment you've got and be creative. Creativity makes the difference between a good skier and a great skier. This is one of my sample fun sessions:

Jump on SB (Page 80)
Cool Board Offset Squats (Page 81)
Tree Climb (Page 81)
Single Leg Obstacle Hops (Page 82)
Slacklining (Page 82)
Lower Abs SB (Page 83)
Washing Machine (Page 83)
Rope Climb (Page 83)

PHASE 6 SAMPLE SCHEDULE

Week	Mon	Tues	Wed	Thurs	Fri	Sat	Sun
1	P6S1		P6S2		P6S1		
2	P6S2	P6S1		P6S2		P6S1	
3			P6S1		P6S2		P6S1
4	P6S1	P6S2		P6S1			

STRETCHING PROGRAMME

You do not stretch to avoid pulling muscles: stretching should be used to re-balance your posture. An optimal posture will ensure the body's joints move around the 'optimal axis of rotation', enabling best performance and reducing the chance of injury. 'Pulled' muscles are a result of poor alignment. With this in mind you do not want to static stretch before a sport/activity because it will not reduce the chance of injury, but it will reduce performance. When you static stretch you take 'tone' out the muscles which in effect, 'puts the muscle to sleep'. However, you do want to warm-up muscles through dynamic (moving) stretching to pump blood into the muscles as per the warm-up/mobilisations in this programme.

Sometimes, in the controlled environment of a 'rehabilitation' training programme, you choose to put over-active, tight muscles to sleep by taking the 'tone' out of the specific muscle by static stretching. This will help you to perform a rehabilitation exercise correctly.

So, it is important to stretch your short tight muscles but not the longer, weaker muscles (which you do want to strengthen and shorten). For example, if your chest muscles are too short, they will pull your shoulders forward, creating longer upper back muscles. In this case you need to stretch your chest muscles and strengthen your upper back muscles. This will optimally align your shoulder girdle.

If you think of your body as a bicycle wheel, the aim is to make sure the spokes are all the right length: not too short or too long, creating the perfect alignment for a smooth ride. This is why a general stretching programme that is not tailored to your unique needs is not a good idea, as you might be stretching muscles that are already too long and weak.

RECOVERY PROGRAMME

Generally, a well-balanced, posture-focused programme using the recommended warm-ups and recovery programmes – like the ones detailed in this book – will go a long way to aligning your body.

I would also highly recommend booking yourself a postural assessment with a suitable health professional* together with a corrective exercise programme of strengthening and stretching according to your specific needs.

**A Chek practitioner is best. Visit www.chekconnect.com*

Note:
Static stretching

- puts muscles to sleep
- do not use before a sport/activity
- use in rehabilitation and after sport/activity

Dynamic Stretching/Mobilisations

- prepares the body for sport/activity by pumping blood to muscles
- use before sport/activity
- can also be used anytime to aid recovery

Sports massage is also recommended.

Recovery Programme can be completed daily. Plan to complete on five days of each week.

First, learn how to diaphragm breathe: breathe in through your nose with your belly coming out, then breathe all the way out (through nose or mouth) with your tummy coming in. It's not easy – practise!

Use this breathing method in the exercises below. They should be very slow. If you are getting out of breath you are going too fast.

RECOVERY CIRCUIT 1 (RC1):

- Breathing Squats (Page 85)
- Pelvic Tilts (Page 86)
- Horse Stance (dynamic) (Page 86)
- Prone Cobra (Page 87)
- Neck Rotations (Page 87)
- Cross Crawl (Page 88)

RECOVERY CIRCUIT 2 (RC2):

- Superman (Page 89)
- Leg Tuck (Page 89)
- Woodchop (Page 90)
- Mackenzie Press-up (Page 90)
- Thoracic Mobilisations (Page 91)
- Alternate Nostril Breathing (Page 91)

About 10 reps or 1 minute on each exercise – there's no need to be precise on the recovery programme.

Overall Schedule (2-5 months)

PHASE 2 (2-4 WEEKS)

Week	Mon	Tues	Wed	Thurs	Fri	Sat	Sun
1	P2S1		P2S1		P2S1		
2	P2S1		P2S1		P2S1		P2S1
3	P2S2	P2S1		P2S1	P2S2		
4	P2S1	P2S2		P2S1	P2S2		

PHASE 3 (6-8 WEEKS)

Week	Mon	Tues	Wed	Thurs	Fri	Sat	Sun
5	P3S1		P3S1		P3S1		
6	P3S1		P3S1		P3S1		
7	P3S1		P3S1		P3S1		
8	P3S2		P3S2		P3S2		
9	P3S1	P3S2		P3S1		P3S2	
10	P3S1	P3S2		P3S1		P3S2	
11	P3S1	P3S2		P3S1		P3S2	
12	P3S1	P3S2		P3S1		P3S2	

PHASE 4 (4 WEEKS) ADVANCED ONLY

Week	Mon	Tues	Wed	Thurs	Fri	Sat	Sun
13	P4S1		P4S1		P4S2		
14	P4S1		P4S2		P4S1		P4S2
15		P4S1	P4S2			P4S1	P4S2
16			P4S1		P4S2		

PHASE 5 (4 WEEKS) FOR ANYONE

Week	Mon	Tues	Wed	Thurs	Fri	Sat	Sun
17	P5C1		P5C1		P5C1		
18	P5C2		P5C2		P5C2		
19	P5C1	P5C2		P5C1	P5C2		
20	P5C1	P5C2		P5C1	P5C2		P5C1

PHASE 6 (4 WEEKS) ATHLETES ONLY

Week	Mon	Tues	Wed	Thurs	Fri	Sat	Sun
17	P6S1		P6S2		P6S1		
18	P6S2	P6S1		P6S2		P6S1	
19			P6S1		P6S2		P6S1
20	P6S1	P6S2		P6S1			

Taper - Ski - Recovery - Ski again

WARM-UPS AND COOL-DOWNS

(DYNAMIC STRETCHING/MOBILISATIONS)

Before and after all sessions and circuits conduct a warm-up/cool-down. Examples of these are:

SB SWINGS

ARM/NECK MOBILISATIONS

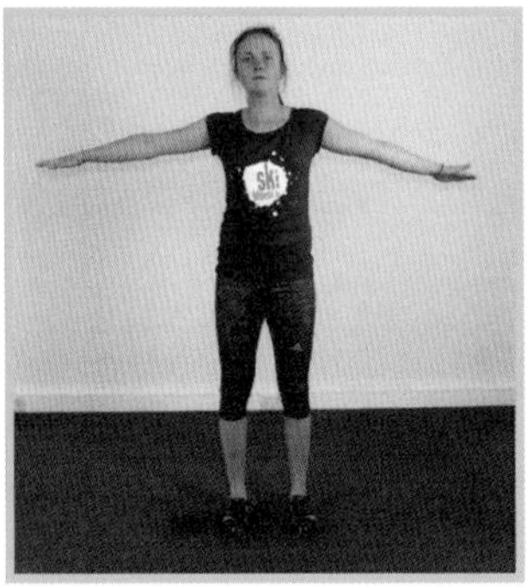

EYGPTIAN SHOULDER/HIP MOBILISATIONS

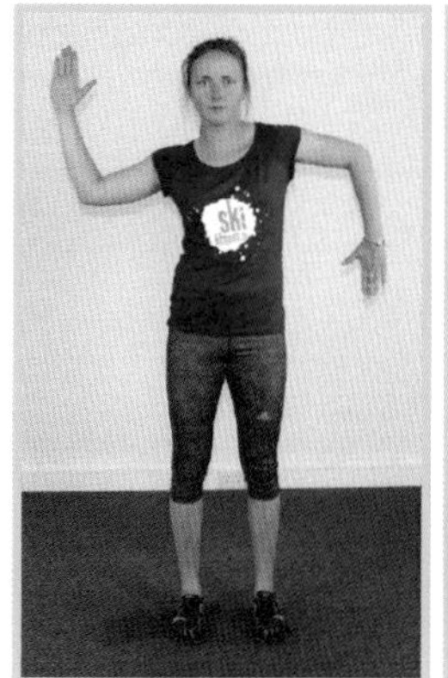

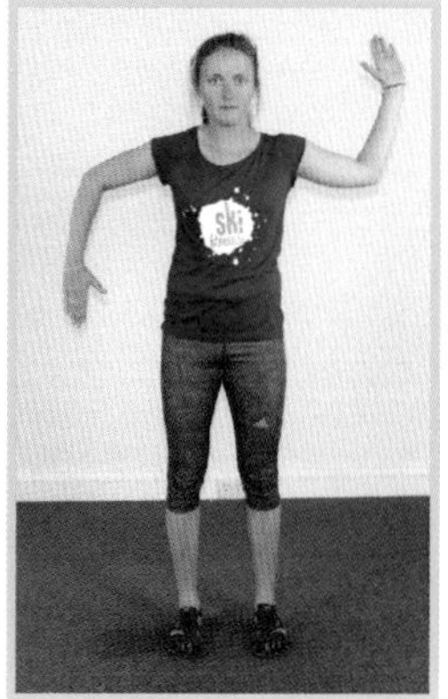

LEG SWINGS – 'HAMY'S & HIPS'

FOAM ROLLER

On anything tight, e.g. calves (you'll know they're tight if they hurt!)

SB BALANCE

Try doing some of the exercises at 50% intensity (for example halving any weights you may be using) as a warm-up or cool-down.

CHAPTER 3

EXERCISE DETAIL

CHAPTER 3

To help you perform each exercise with perfect technique, this section details the exercises including photos. There are also videos available online at www.skifitness.tv.

Descriptions:
- Why
- How
- Progressions
- Outdoor alternative

P2S1 PHASE 2 SESSION 1

SINGLE LEG SHIN/TOE TOUCHES

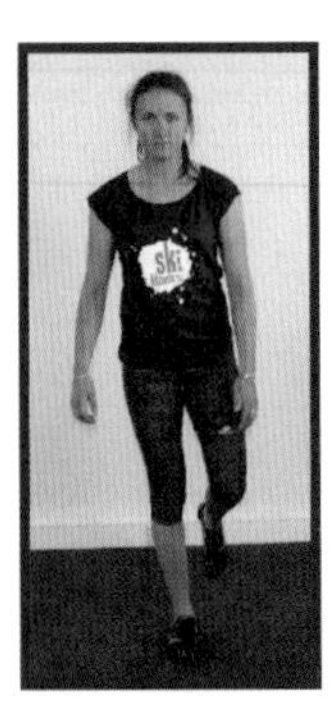

Single Leg Shin/ Toe Touches	1	8 each side	Bodyweight (BW)	-

Why: Improves balance and stabilisation around key joints such as ankle, knee, hips. Links the upper and lower body in a functional twist movement.

How: Stand on one leg and touch your shin or toes with opposite hand.

Progressions: Touch lower down, keep spine neutral/straight (see Chapter 4), add weight in hand, stand on balance aid (BOSU, balance disc).

BALL ROLLOUTS

Ball Rollouts	4-10	10 secs	Tech.	10 secs

Why: Links upper and lower body and stabilises your inner core. You can adjust pressure to ensure perfect technique thereby recruiting the key inner core stabilisers. If it's too hard you'll revert to the bad habits of recruiting your outer core only.
(See section 4 on Core.)

How: Kneel on the mat with your elbows on a stability ball. Move your body forward ensuring the angles at your shoulders and hips are the same. Hold for 10 seconds in a position where you can feel the activation of your tummy muscles but no aching or pain in your lower back.

Progressions: Imagine your elbows are a pencil and move them to 'draw' letters and words.

LOWER ABDOMINAL 1-4

LA1

LA2

Hand Position

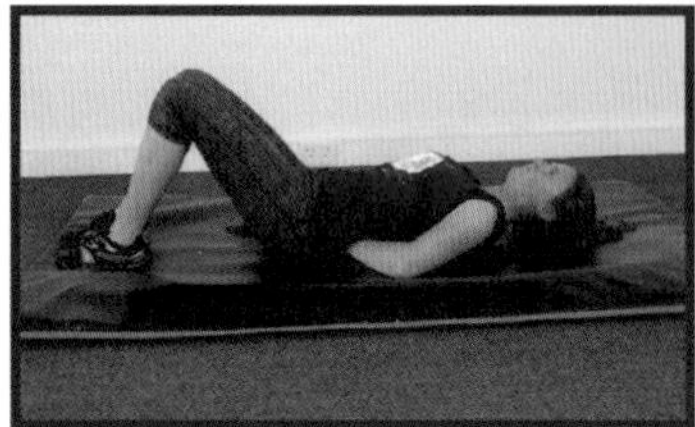

LA3

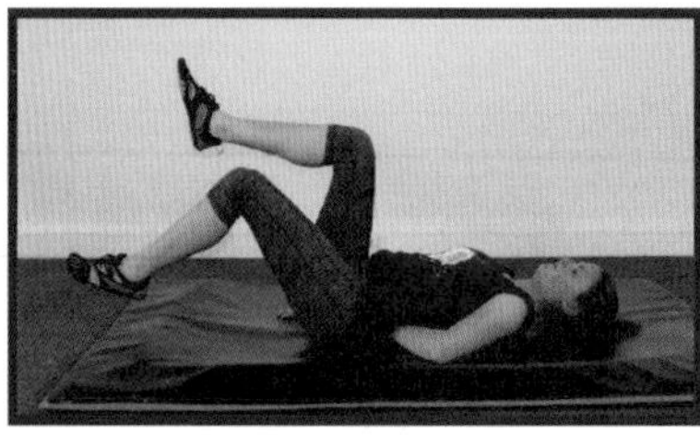

LA3

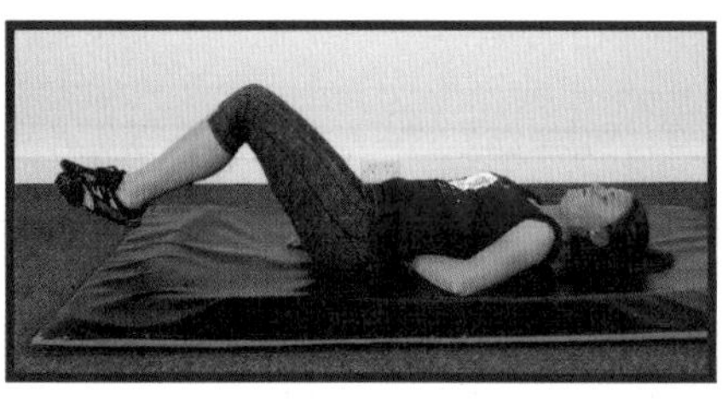

LA4

LA1-4	4-10	10-20 secs	Tech.	20 secs

Why: This exercise is designed to see if you have the core coordination and control to choose what position to put the rest of your body in. A force will come from an extremity (legs or arms) into your core. The response from your core will then decide the best position for your extremities to deal with the next force. If you have no core control, your spine will move in time with your extremity and will not be able to choose the best position, for example, keeping your knee in line with your feet. This will lead to reduced efficiency (fitness), poor performance and injury. This is an 'isolation exercise' to rehabilitate the core, which means you need to be able to perform it well, but once you can perform it, you do not need to do the exercise anymore as it will be incorporated in more functional exercises (see Chapter 4).

How: Lie with your back on the floor. Place the widest part of one hand facing down, in the small of your back, directly behind your tummy button. Bring both legs up, off the floor with your knees at right angles. Draw your tummy button down by about one third (naval towards spine) and flatten back into your hand with about 50% pressure. Move legs, keeping 90 degrees at the knee towards the floor, maintaining that 50% pressure on your hand.

For more accuracy than just feeling pressure on your hand, you can use a pressure cuff (such as one for measuring blood pressure, called a sphygmomanometer, which is easy and cheap to purchase online but not easy to pronounce). Use the pressure cuff instead of your hand, pumping it to 40 bar of pressure and then add another 30 bar by pressing your lower back down into the cuff for the exercise – so keep at 70 bar. (If you have a flat lower back pump to 70 bar and keep at 100 bar).

Progressions (and Regressions):

LA1 – Feet on floor with no leg movement
LA2 – One leg in air, one leg on floor, one leg moving
LA3 – Two legs in air but only one leg moving at a time
LA4 – Two legs in air, two legs moving (as above and test level)
LA5 – Same as above but standing
LA6 – On floor but with straight legs

P2S2 PHASE 2 SESSION 2

SQUATS

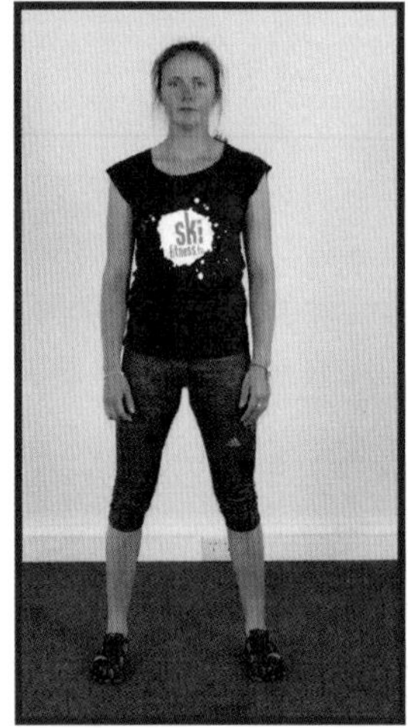

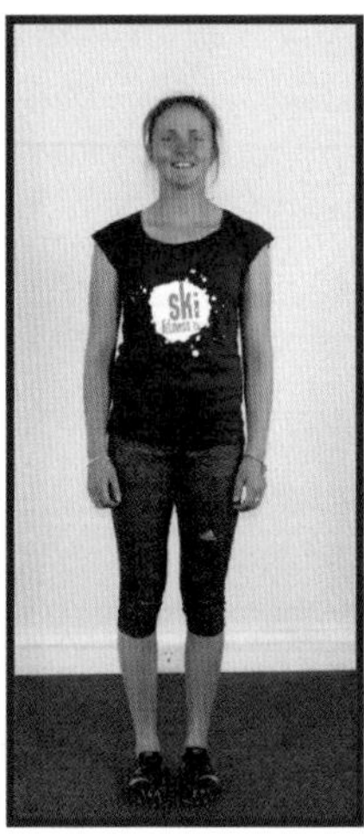

Squats	1-2	10-12	BW	1:00

Why: The best ever conditioning exercise, and ideal for skiing. Uses at least 70% of the body's muscles especially the core, glutes (gluteals or your 'butt' if American) and thighs (quads). It is very important to do this exercise correctly.

How: Stand with your feet shoulder width apart. Initiate squat movement by imagining you are 'sitting down into a chair', leading with your bottom not your knees. Keep even distribution of your weight on your heels and the balls of your feet. Keep your spine straight/neutral (but don't confuse this with being upright - see Chapter 4).

Go as low as you feel comfortable but an average squat would be to bend 90 degrees at the knee. If you feel pain in your knees (or anywhere else) you are doing it incorrectly. Return to the upright position.

Progressions: Cross arms with hands on shoulders, keeping arms horizontal throughout the movement. Draw your tummy button in by one third as you go down (activating your core muscles); release on way up. Add a barbell/weight across your shoulders or dumbbells in your hands.

LATERAL LUNGES

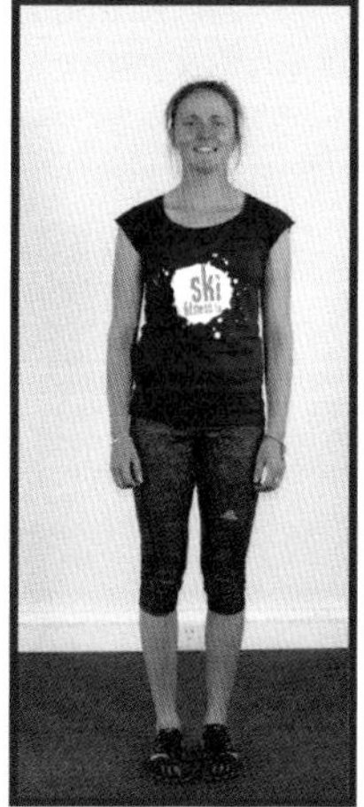

X – incorrect: knee not in line with toes

Lateral Lunges	1-2	16-20	BW	1:00

Why: Like the squat, the lunge uses the key skiing muscles of the legs in integration with the upper body through the core. Lateral lunges also give a different plane of motion – side to side (frontal plane).

How: Stand upright with your legs together. Step out a good stride length to one side. Your weight should be 70% over your leading leg, knee at right angles and in line with your toes. Your following leg should be nearly straight. Look up, with your neutral spine and hands forward. Then step back to the start position and repeat on the other side.

Progressions: Don't progress too quickly, instead, work on your technique. Hold weights or a medicine ball in your hands. Go in multi-directions (see later programmes).

BALL PLANK

Ball Plank	1-4	10-20 secs	BW	0:20

Why: To stabilise the core by making it work to hold the upper and lower body in line under a controlled pressure. Also helps stabilise and strengthen the shoulder (rotator cuff) muscles, which is very important as the shoulder is such a mobile joint. It is an isometric exercise which means your muscles are working hard but are not moving.

How: Put your feet on a stability ball and your hands on the floor in a press-up position. Hold your body in-line for the duration of the exercise (10-20 seconds). Neutral spine. You can use a broomstick to check your position is correct. The broomstick should be level, with your bottom, upper back and head all touching the broom. The gap/curve in your back should be the width of your hand (about 1 inch for most people) and your chin should be tucked in (as if you could hold a tennis ball in place under your chin).

Progressions: If your alignment/posture is poor you will be strengthening and reinforcing this poor posture, leading to reduced performance and injury – so work on your alignment as detailed above before you progress. You can increase the duration of the exercise up to two minutes.

SB SUPINE OFFSETS

Offset Right

Offset Left

Pole added to help alignment

SB Supine Offsets	1-2	10	BW	1:00

Why: Stabilises core in frontal plane and is an excellent exercise for strengthening the back and activating the glutes.

How: Start by sitting on a stability ball, then walk forward until your head and shoulders come to rest on the ball. Keep your hips up and your feet shoulder-width apart. Then move your shoulders to one side with one shoulder coming off the ball. Hold this position for three seconds and then move slowly to the other side repeating the hold. There will be a tendency for your inside hip (the left hip if you move to the right) to drop, so check this and make sure both hips stay level.

Progressions: You can go across a little further and hold a little longer.

SB WALL PRESS

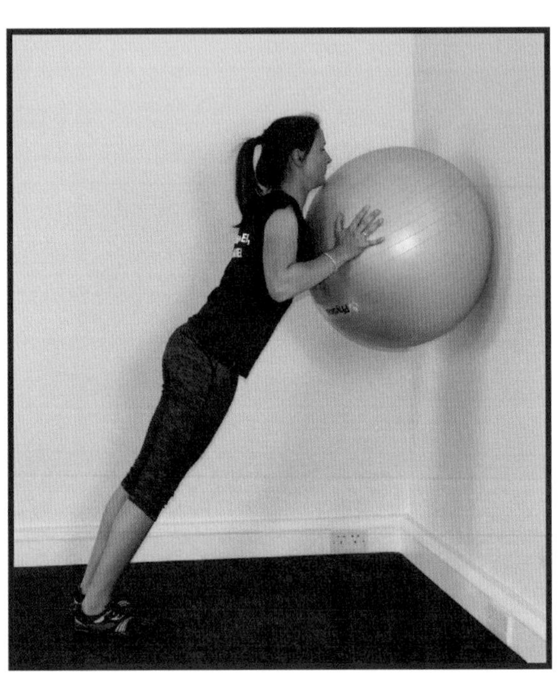

SB Wall Press	1-2	10-12	BW	1:00

Why: It works the front of your body, chest, shoulders, back of arms, and the all-important core.

How: Position a stability ball on a wall in front of you. Place your hands in an outwards position on the ball and lower your chest (not head) to the ball until it nearly touches. It is fine for your heels to come up. You might have to adjust your foot position and ball height to make it hard enough to work the muscles, but not so hard that your hips drop or you cannot get your chest to the ball.

Progressions: Place your feet further back; place the ball lower on the wall; place the ball on the floor wedged into wall; place the ball freestanding on the floor.

P3S1 PHASE 3 SESSION 1

FRONT SQUAT

Front Squat	2-4	8-10	2RR	2:00	212

Why: The squat is a key conditioning exercise, helping strengthen the whole body in a functional and ski-specific way. It is a great core exercise as well as for the legs. If you are familiar with the back squat, the front squat is harder and so the weight you can lift on a front squat will be about 70% of your weight on the back squat. It activates the core well.

How: Ideally, pick up a barbell from a rack with your forearms crossed. Place the tips of your fingers on your shoulders, your arms parallel to the ground. The bar should rest on your shoulders just in front of your neck. You can hold the bar lightly with your fingers but as you squat down, work your core hard to keep the arms parallel with the ground and if you succeed in this, the bar will stay on your shoulders. The weight of the bar might cause a little pressure pain on the first go but will subside once the muscles are used to it. (If this 'pressure point' pain carries on more than a couple of goes, do not ignore it: get professional advice).

See 'Squat' instructions from Phase 2 above. The bar should stay within the distance covered by the length of your feet as it moves up and down. The bar going in front of your feet could be due to a misalignment of your spine or lack of core support. As always seek the advice of a Chek Practitioner (www.chekconnect.com) if unsure. The bar behind your feet means you are too upright or you've fallen over!

If you don't have a barbell you can use dumbbells in you hands.

Progressions: Increase the weight of the barbell; squat lower but listen to your body and don't force it if in pain – remember technique is everything.

Outdoor alternative: Any weight will do such as a rock, the kids, etc.

PULL-UP/BODY ROW

Pull-up/ Body Row	1-3	8-10	1RR	1:00	112

Why: Pull exercises are essential for a balanced programme. They work the upper back muscles (which are often ignored in programmes) and will help with 'rounded-shoulders posture' from too much sitting. Being a body-weight exercise, they use the body functionally, in particular engaging the core. They also help catch wayward button lifts!

How: Find a bar, a tree or TRX. Pull either your whole bodyweight or have the bar low enough to keep your feet on the ground. Vary hand grip: overhand (breathe-in on pull); underhand (breathe-out on pull); offset grip (breathe anyhow). Breathing correctly helps activate the muscles you are trying to work. Complete the full range of motion with your arms going totally straight on the way back.

Progressions: Body row to pull-up; increase reps; vary grip; weighted belt; one arm; offset bar (use natural bars such as branches).

Outdoor alternative: Tree, TRX, rope, playground, a table at a push.

CABLE PRESS

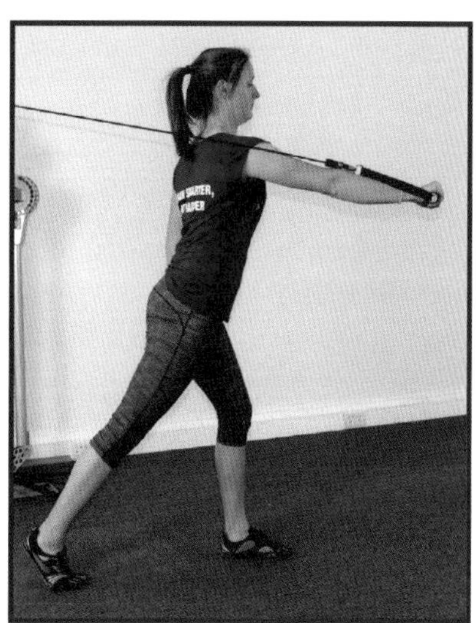

Cable Press	1-3	8-10 each arm	2RR	1:00	112

Why: Press exercises are a part of a balanced functional programme. A cable press as opposed to a bench press is more functional (and therefore better for skiing, sport and life in general) because it engages the core, adds a twist pattern and is in the standing position.

How: A cable machine is great because it fits you rather than you having to fit the machine, however this means you receive no alignment help so you need to make sure you stay aware and in control of the alignment of your whole body during the movement. Start in an offset 'archery' stance: if you have your left foot forward, use your right hand to hold the handle next to your shoulder with your elbow up and your palm facing down. Start activation at your left foot, then your core, turning your hips 90 degrees, and then punch through with right hand in a smooth, dynamic and powerful movement. Breathe out, lift your right heel and stabilise on your left foot as you punch, then return to the start position inhaling. Your forearm, wrist and knuckles should always be in line with the cable. You should feel your core stabilising like in a plank but this time, exercising and moving as well! Keep you shoulder down throughout the movement.

This is not an easy exercise to perform correctly so start with a low weight and progress slowly.

Progressions: Not really necessary, but you could have fun by standing on a BOSU or stability disk; switch your stance; kneel/stand on Swiss ball; change the cable height.

CHEK SHOULDER PRESS

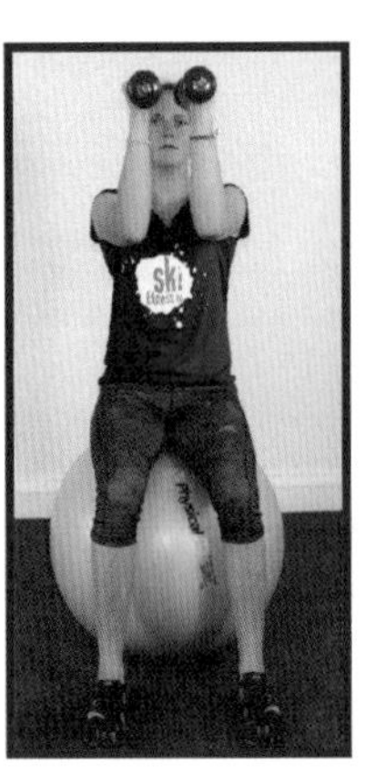

Chek Shoulder Press	1-3	8-10	2RR	1:00	2322

Why: The shoulder is a fantastically mobile joint and is supported/controlled by four main rotator cuff muscles. The relationship between the length and tension of these muscles is imperative to maintain (or reinstate) good balance. The Chek press helps do this through its unusual rotating movement.

How: Sit on a stability ball. Choose two light dumbbells. Start with your upper arms out to the side of the body parallel to the floor with a 90 degree bend at the elbow. Bring your arms into the centre towards each other, keeping the forearms parallel with each other. Press upwards, working to keep the elbows within the width of the shoulders until your arms are straight above your head. Rotate your arms out and lower back to the start position.

Progressions: Reverse the movement by pushing straight up as in a normal shoulder press. Bring your elbows parallel and lower your arms while keeping your elbows within the width of your shoulders.

Home alternative: use wine bottles instead of dumbbells (septuagenarian programme tester recommended table white!)

RUSSIAN TWIST

MB added

Russian Twist	1-3	8-10	1RR	1:00	Fluid

Why: I was once told that any exercise with an Eastern European or Russian sounding name was always going to be good! Also, it is relatively simple, engages balance, can be controlled or dynamic and is obviously a twist pattern, which is crucial for skiing. Twist is both a plane of motion and a key functional movement pattern (see Chapter4).

How: Place your feet on floor, your head and shoulders on a Swiss ball and your arms straight up with your hands together over the centre of your chest. Keep your tongue in roof of mouth (say 'the' and you'll have it) to stabilise the neck muscles. Keeping your hips up and as level as possible, twist your upper body to one side a full 90 degrees so your arms point sideways. The ball should move underneath you, with one shoulder on the ball and one directly above the other. Your arms should stay straight with your hands staying directly in line with the chest. Move your head in line with your arms. If you fall off, well done for trying! It's not that far to fall, so try again focusing on getting the ball to move so you stay directly above it. Return to the starting position and go to the other side.

Progressions: Use a medicine ball or hold a weight in your hands; make the movement more dynamic (faster); keep the head pointing upwards (not moving with hands).

LOWER ABDOMINAL 1-4

LA1

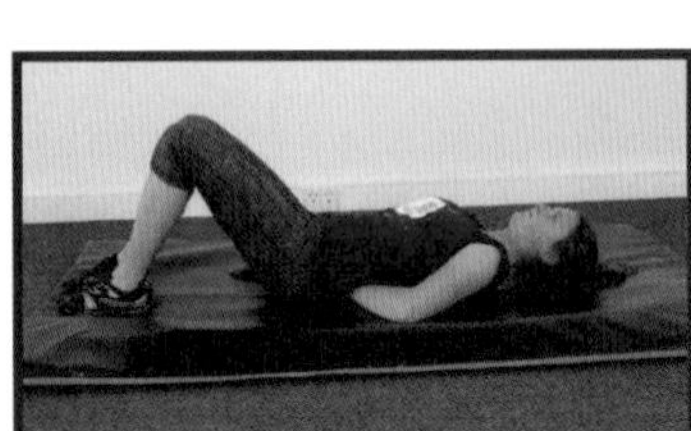

LA2

Hand Position

LA3

LA3

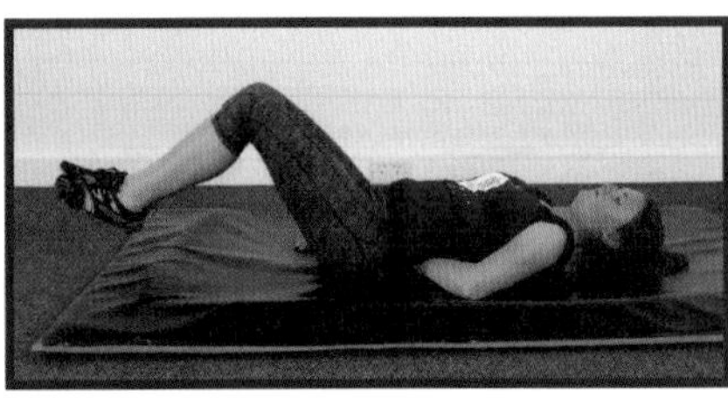

LA4

LA1-4	4-10	10-20 secs	Tech.	20 secs

See page 35 for instructions

P3S2 PHASE 3 SESSION 2

DEADLIFT

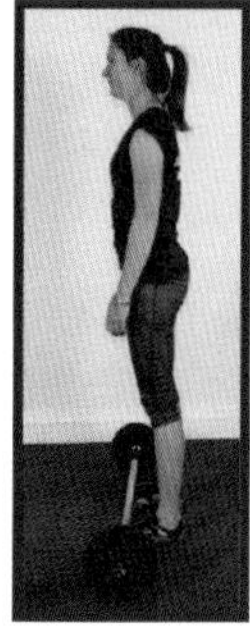

Deadlift	2-4	8-10	2RR	2:00	212

Why: To activate and strengthen hamstrings, glutes and back. Very functional. It is similar, but subtly different, from the squat. It works the back of your thighs (hamstrings), more than the front of your thighs (quads).

How: Approach a barbell with your feet slightly wider than shoulder width apart. Bend over with a neutral (straight) spine and hold the barbell with an overhand grip (or one overhand one underhand for better grip) close to your legs. Keep your knees slightly bent but stationary. Ensure that there is some convex curve in your lower back, then engage the core (draw-in your tummy button by about one third), and activate the glutes (by thinking about these muscles). In a powerful movement, lift up the bar, hinging from the hip and stand straight upright. Lower the bar as far as you can go without moving at the knees or losing the convex curve in your lower back. Then perform the next repetition. Do not let the weight pull your arms forward, losing your upper back neutral spine posture. If the bar is lifted from the floor and that is too low for a perfected technique as described above, then bend the knees more on the first lift or raise the bar onto blocks. You can use dumbbells instead.

Progressions: There are many and varied progressions to this exercise, but at this stage it is best to stick to perfecting this version.

Outdoor Alternative: Use a rock or other heavy object.

MULTI-D LUNGES

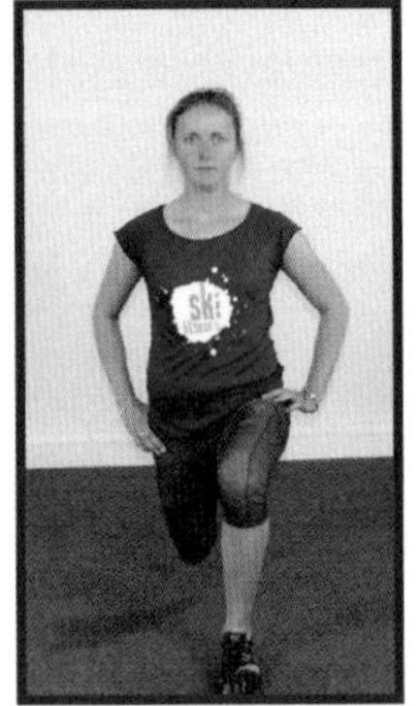

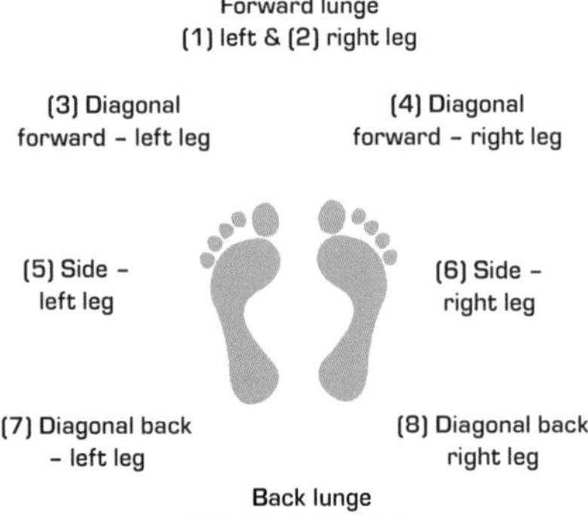

Multi-d Lunges	1-3	20	1RR	1:00	112

Why: The lunge is a key functional movement pattern with obvious benefits for skiing. It uses key skiing muscles in the legs and core as well as challenging balance and alignment. This multi-directional lunge also incorporates two planes of motion – saggital (forward and backward) and frontal (side to side).

How: Think of a compass rose. Step forward with left leg to the North. Keep the weight on the heel of your left foot with your knee in line with your toes. Your right foot heel can lift up, with the right knee nearly touching the ground. Push off from the front/left heel and return to the starting position then lunge to the North with the right leg. Next, lunge towards the North West with left foot, keeping your weight through heel, and your knee in line with your toes. Key point: Your right thigh should still point North and you should feel your inner thighs working. Lunge back and repeat with the right foot to the North East. Then, repeat with the left foot to West, keeping both feet pointing forward (North), with your left leg bent to 90 degrees and with 70% weight through the left foot. Your right leg stays straight-ish. Then repeat with the right foot to the East and back; left foot to the South West and back; right foot South East and back; left foot South and then right foot South. Engage your core at the furthest point of each lunge and maintain a neutral spine throughout. You can reverse process to come back to North.

Progressions: Make the process more dynamic (faster); hold a weight; play around with the order and angle of lunge.

MB REVERSE WOODCHOP

MB Reverse Woodchop	1-3	8-10 each side	2RR	1:00	112

Why: This is a twist pattern, is good for upper back posture, and strengthens back and core in a whole-body movement.

How: Hold a medicine ball in your hands. Lower the ball to the side of one knee in a half-squat (keeping your spine neutral and knees in line with toes). Swing the ball up across your body, keeping arms straight and end up with the ball above your head on the other side from where you started. Return slowly to the start position and repeat to complete the set. Then swap to the other side.

This involves extension and rotation of the lumbar spine (lower back) which is, potentially, quite stressful on the body, especially if you lack strength and alignment in this area (which you will be made aware of by pain signals). Start off with a low weight and slow movement and progress gradually.

Progressions: Increase speed and weight; change the shape of the weight eg: a kettlebell or cable machine.

Outdoor Alternative: The weight could be a rock or a weighted rucksack.

Weighted rucksack

ONE ARM CABLE PULL

One Arm Cable Pull	1-3	8-10 each arm	2RR	Ø	2322

Why: It works the upper back in a 'pull and twist' functional pattern. It is very good for upper back posture (a common problem).

How: This is the opposite action to the cable push. Using one arm at a time, face the cable in an 'archery' stance. With your palm facing down, 'draw'/pull the cable back, keeping knuckles, wrist, arm and elbow all in-line with the cable. Make sure you complete the full range of motion in this exercise by finishing the pull with the scapula (shoulder blade) moving back and down across the back. Do not let your elbow drop or your shoulders rise. Keep a continuous, smooth and powerful movement back then slowly return to the start point. Inhale as you pull back, and exhale as you return to activate the correct muscles. Remember, as with the cable push, you need to control your movements and stabilise your posture.

Progressions: None yet.

Outdoor: Suspension strap e.g. TRX, body row (pull-up with feet on ground) on bar, branch etc.

BALL PRESS-UPS (WALL)

Ball Press-ups (Wall)	1-3	8-10	1RR	1:00	Fluid

Why: This exercise works the chest, core and shoulders in a functional pattern.

How: Place a stability ball on the wall at about shoulder height. Hold the stability ball with both hands, fingers pointing sideways to take pressure off the wrists. Keep your feet on floor with legs straight – your heels can come up. Lower your chest until it nearly touches the ball, then push back to straight arms, in the start position. Engage your core, keep your spine neutral, do not let your hips drop as you push back. Inhale as you go down, exhale as you push back.

Progressions: Ball wedged between floor and wall; ball on the floor in the open.

SB SUPINE OFFSET LEG-LIFT

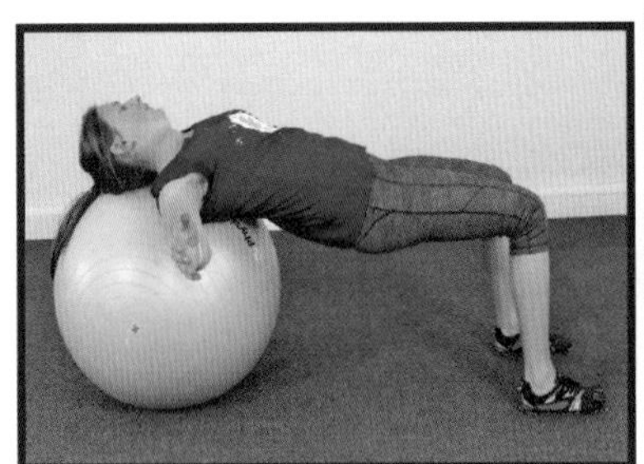

SB Supine Offset Leg-lift	1-2	10	BW	1:00	333

Why: This exercise works the back in connection with the glutes, legs and shoulders. It is a frontal plane (side to side) movement often overlooked in many gym programmes and is very important for skiing. It works the contrasting forces of stability and movement.

How: Start in a bridge position facing upwards (supine) with your head and shoulders on a stability ball, and your feet shoulder width apart on the floor with your knees directly above your feet. Offset by moving your body to the right with your right shoulder just coming off the ball support, then lift your left leg off the floor by extending at the knee. Keep your hips up and level and your knees in line with each other. Hold, and then return your foot to floor. Move body back into the middle of the ball and repeat, moving left this time and lifting your right leg.

Progressions: Go further out; hold for longer; supporting foot on stability disc.

PRONE FEET BALL ROLL

Prone Feet Ball Roll	1-2	20	BW	1:00	Fluid

Why: This is a great core exercise contrasting the forces of stability and movement. It works on the balance and twist pattern.

How: Place your feet/legs on the stability ball, and your hands on the ground in a facing down (prone) position. Keep your hips up and a neutral spine throughout. Twist hips/legs side to side. Start off with only small movements.

Progressions: A ball can be placed on the knees, shins, feet or toes getting progressively harder. Increase movement (side to side distance) and speed of movement.

P4S1 PHASE 4 SESSION 1

BB CLEAN & PRESS

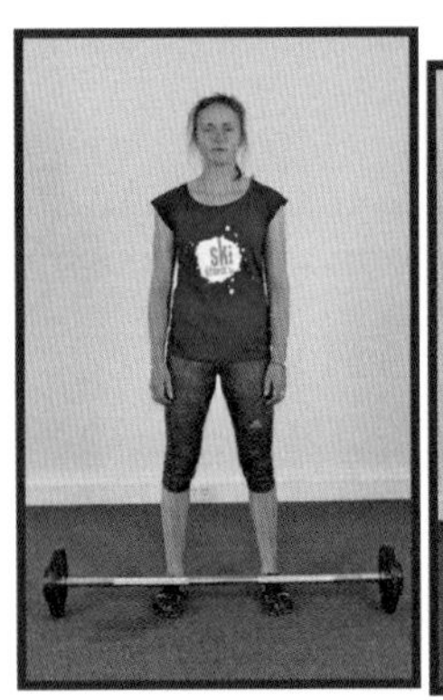

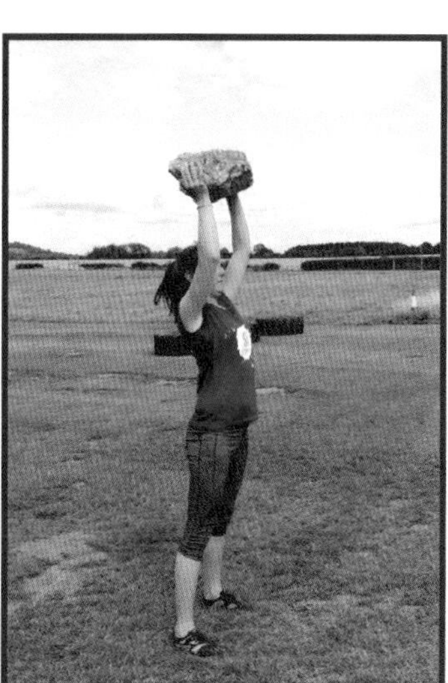

BB Clean & Press	3-5	8-10	1RR	3:00	Fast

Why: This progresses the strength programme by linking upper and lower body movement patterns and introducing power (power = speed and strength). It is a total body exercise using most of the body's muscles in a functional way.

How: Stand behind a barbell on the floor, and bend at the hips and knees to grip the barbell just wider than your shoulders. Explosively extend your legs then drive your hips forward and shrug your shoulders to pull the bar upward. Drop under the bar to catch the bar at shoulder height with your knees bent. Extend your legs again and power-press your arms straight overhead. Slowly return to the start position and repeat.
Progressions: Work on your technique first but you can increase weight and speed. Use one leg one arm with a DB.

Outdoor: Use a rock, log, weighted bag or similar.

CABLE JUMP TWIST

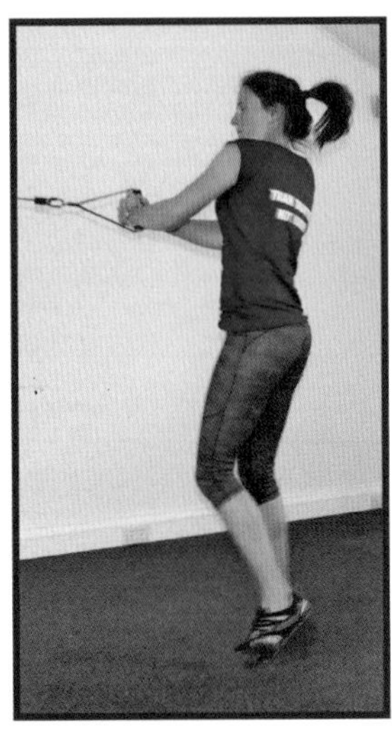

Cable Jump Twist	3	30	High	Ø	Fast

Why: This exercise introduces explosive power and dynamic balance to a twist movement pattern.

How: Set the cable at shoulder height. Stand sideways-on to the cable and hold the handle in both hands out in front, with your knees slightly bent, and a neutral spine. Explosively jump 180 degrees drawing the cable horizontally across body to the far shoulder. Keep your arms straight (without elbows locking-out). Jump 180 degrees back to the starting position. Repeat. Each jump is one repetition.

Progressions: Faster; better technique; one leg.

Outdoor alternative: Use a bungee on a tree.

SINGLE LEG SQUATS (BENCH)

Single Leg Squats (Bench)	3	8-10 each leg	1RR	2:00	Controlled

Why: Much of skiing uses one leg more than the other, so training on one leg ensures strength and stability of each leg independently.

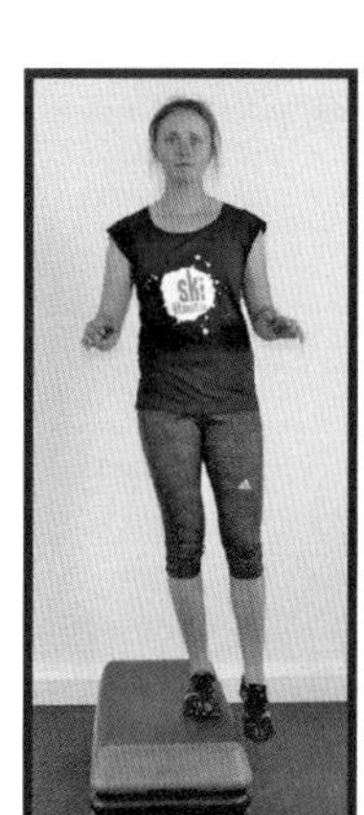

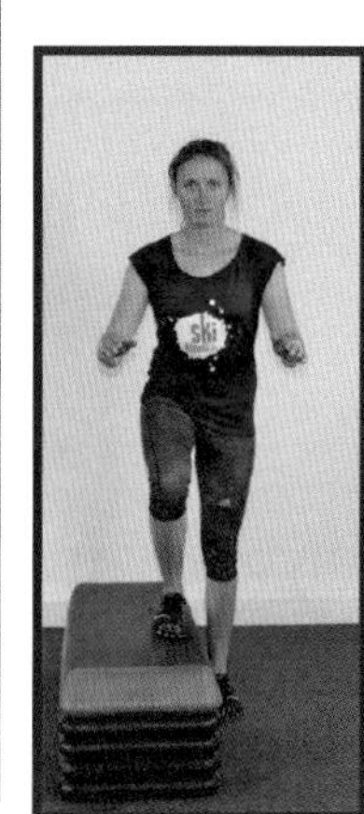

How: Stand one-legged on a bench and then lower the other leg until you lightly touch the floor with your toes, then return to standing. Initiate movement with your bottom, sitting down into the movement. Your upper body comes forward, but as always, your spine remains neutral. Your weight stays on the heel and ball of the foot that is on the bench. The bench leg knee stays in line with second toe. There should be no pain in the knee. It should be your thigh, glutes and core that feel like they are working. This is a key exercise and is easy to get wrong, so work on your technique.

Progressions: Slow down the movement; hold at low position for longer; use a higher bench; hold weight in hands (eg: DBs).

Regression: Try on the floor without a step/bench and just bend the other leg. If you are struggling to keep your knee in line with second toe, you can use a stick in your hand and/or press the unweighted knee laterally into a wall. Also, activate your core more and close your hips, ie: rotate hips towards weighted leg.

Outdoor alternative: Practise off a step.

BODY ROW OR PULL-UPS

Body Row (or Pull-ups)	2-3	10-15	High	Ø	Fast

Why: Body weight exercises are always good, very functional and use the core. The 'row' movement pattern strengthens the – often under-trained – back muscles as well as the biceps.

How: Set a bar about chest height. If you have a squat rack you can use an unweighted barbell for this – alternatively you can use rings/TRX or an assisted chin-up machine. Hold the bar slightly wider than your shoulder width with an overhand grip. Walk your legs underneath the bar until your heels are on ground with your toes up (to make it easier, keep your feet flat on the floor with your legs bent). Keep your body straight and pull your chest to the bar and then return to straight arms.

Progressions: Feet on stability disc or BOSU; pull-ups.

Outdoor alternative: TRX, rope, trees, playgrounds.

HANDS ON SB PRESS-UPS

Hands on SB Press-ups	2-3	8-10	High	1:00	Fast

Why: This press pattern gives lots of core and shoulder joint stability.

How: Grasp a stability ball with both hands, fingers pointed laterally (taking pressure of your wrists). Stabilise your core and keep a neutral spine, then lower your chest to the ball and press your back up, keeping the body straight. Be careful not to let your hips drop in and your lower back over-arch.

Progressions: Feet on stability disc or stability ball.

Regressions: Ball in corner of floor and wall; ball on wall.

Outdoor alternative: Take the ball outside or improvise on a branch/tree trunk.

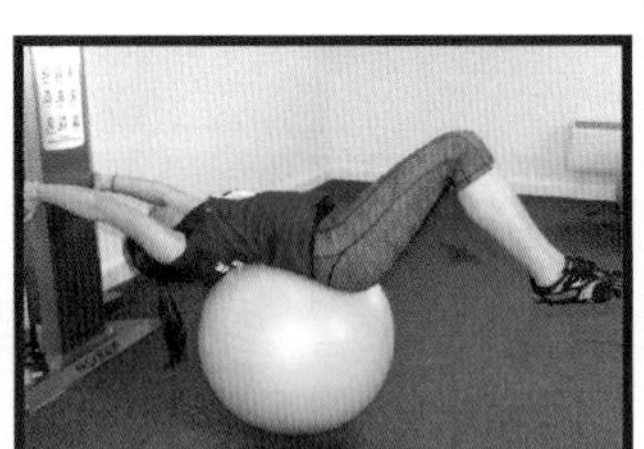

Legs to side

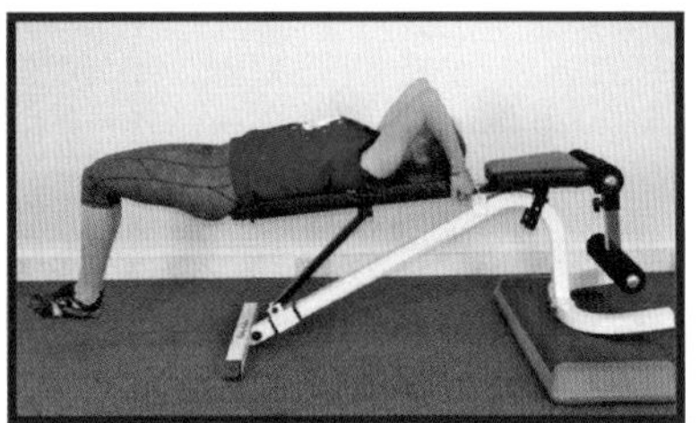

SB LOWER ABS DYNAMIC

SB Lower Abs Dynamic	2-3	10	High	Ø	

Why: Non-moving/stable upper body and dynamic lower body moving is a great core exercise for skiing.

How: Position the small of your back on a stability ball, bring your legs up with knees at 90 degrees and hold an anchor of some description (bench, cable machine) to stabilise your position. It might take a couple of attempts to find the correct position. Keep your head level and your tongue in the roof of your mouth to stabilise your neck. Lower your legs from the hips, keeping knees at 90 degrees until your toes nearly touch the floor and then return your legs to the start position.

Progressions: Vary the speed and then angle of legs.

SB MB POWER SIT-UPS

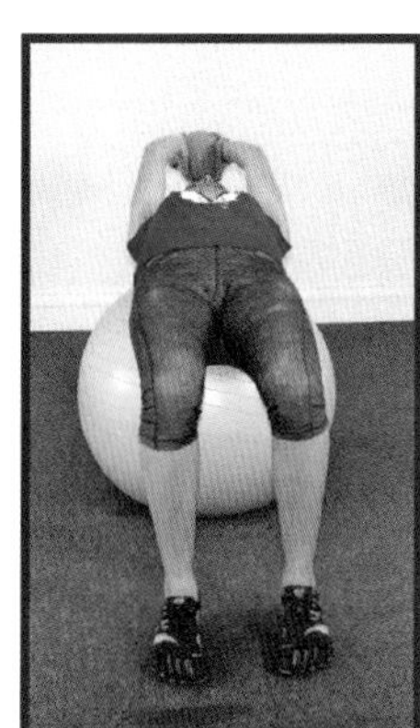

SB MB Power Sit-ups	2-3	10	High	1:00	

Why: This exercise improves core strength and power, activates balance and stability and allows a full range of extension (going back over the ball). Ideally, you need a friend for this one, but if you do not have one handy, you can just keep hold of the ball instead.

How: Position the small of your back on a stability ball with your feet on the ground. Keep your tongue in roof of your mouth. Catch a medicine ball from a partner, and take your arms and body back over the ball to just past horizontal level. From this position sit up and throw the ball back to your partner. The stability ball should not move. It might take a couple of practices with your partner, using a light ball to start with.

Progressions: Heavier ball thrown harder; change trajectory of ball throwing.

P4S2 PHASE 4 SESSION 2

SINGLE ARM DB SNATCH

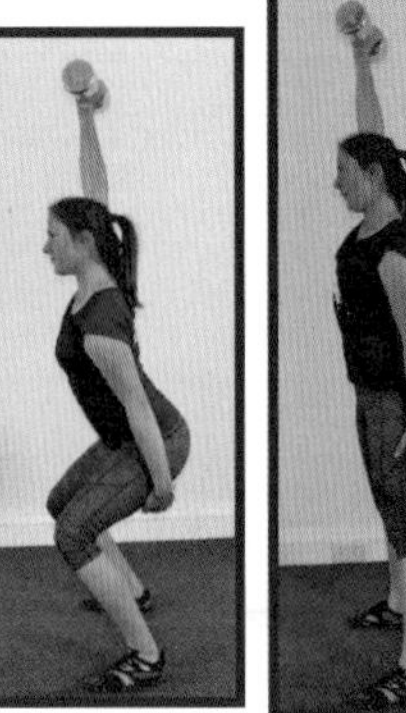

Single Leg

Single Arm DB Snatch	3-5	8-10 - Swap hands half way through	1RR	3:00	Fast

Why: This exercise facilitates fast and powerful total body movement incorporating explosive leg movements and the glutes. The arm/back-pull improves core power and core and shoulder stabilisation. It is an attack on the body that will get it ready for anything the slopes throw at it especially on the one leg progression.

How: Stand behind a DB on the floor, bend at the hips and knees, and using an overhand grip, hold the DB between your feet, with one hand. Explosively extend your legs, drive your hips forward and shrug your shoulders to pull the DB upwards. Drop under the DB to catch it with a straight arm while descending into a squat and then return to standing. Slowly return to the start position and repeat.

Progressions: Single leg; stand on stability ball.

CABLE SINGLE LEG SINGLE ARM PRESS

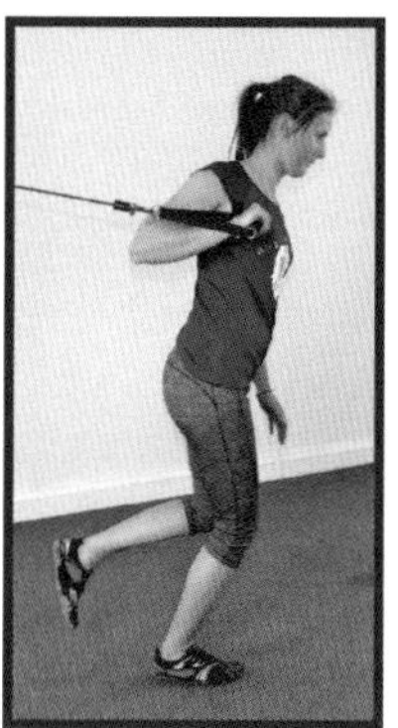

Why: This is a press and twist pattern while stabilising on one leg, and is similar to a ski pole plant.

How: It is the same as the cable press (see Programme 3.1) but you stand on one leg pressing the opposite arm.

Progressions: One leg on BOSU, use leg on the same side as your arm.

Outdoor alternative: One arm press-up; TRX two arm press.

Cable Single Leg Single Press	3	8-10 each side	High	Ø	Fast

CABLE SINGLE LEG SQUAT & SINGLE ARM PULL

Cable Single Leg Squat & Single Arm Pull	2-3	8-10 each side	High	1:00	Fast

Why: These exercises develop the strength built-up in simple movement patterns into more complex and ski-specific total body movement patterns. They strengthen the body to extend through a ski turn, the arm weight (cable) replicating momentum force in a downhill direction.

How: Lower the cable arm to near the floor. Stand on one leg and hold the cable in your opposite hand. Complete a single leg squat (see 4.1), keeping your arm straight, your knee in line with your second toe and your spine neutral. Go as low as you can while keeping this alignment. Extend your leg and draw back your arm, keeping your elbow and forearm in line with the cable (elbow high but with shoulders down). Return to the start (squat position) and repeat.

Progressions: One leg on BOSU; same leg, same arm.

Outdoor alternative: One arm, one leg body row on a tree branch or TRX.

MB WASHING MACHINE

MB Washing Machine	2-3	30-60	High	Ø	Fast

Why: This is a dynamic core twist replicating a twist skiing pattern. How far you twist is generally not how flexible you are, but about how far your body will let you go, knowing it can stop the momentum force and bring you back to neutral without being injured. Building dynamic twist strength will also increase your range of motion and flexibility.

How: Stand with your feet slightly wider than shoulder width. Cuddle a medicine ball tight into your body between your chest and chin. Rotate side to side (180 degrees) as fast as you can (think about the movement of a washing machine drum). Lift your heel slightly to take pressure off the knee. This exercise is harder than it looks, so start slowly with a light MB and build-up the tempo.

Progressions: Use an awkward size and weight to replace the MB; stand on one leg.

Outdoor alternative: Use a rock or log instead of MB.

LATERAL DYNAMIC LUNGES WITH MB LOOPS

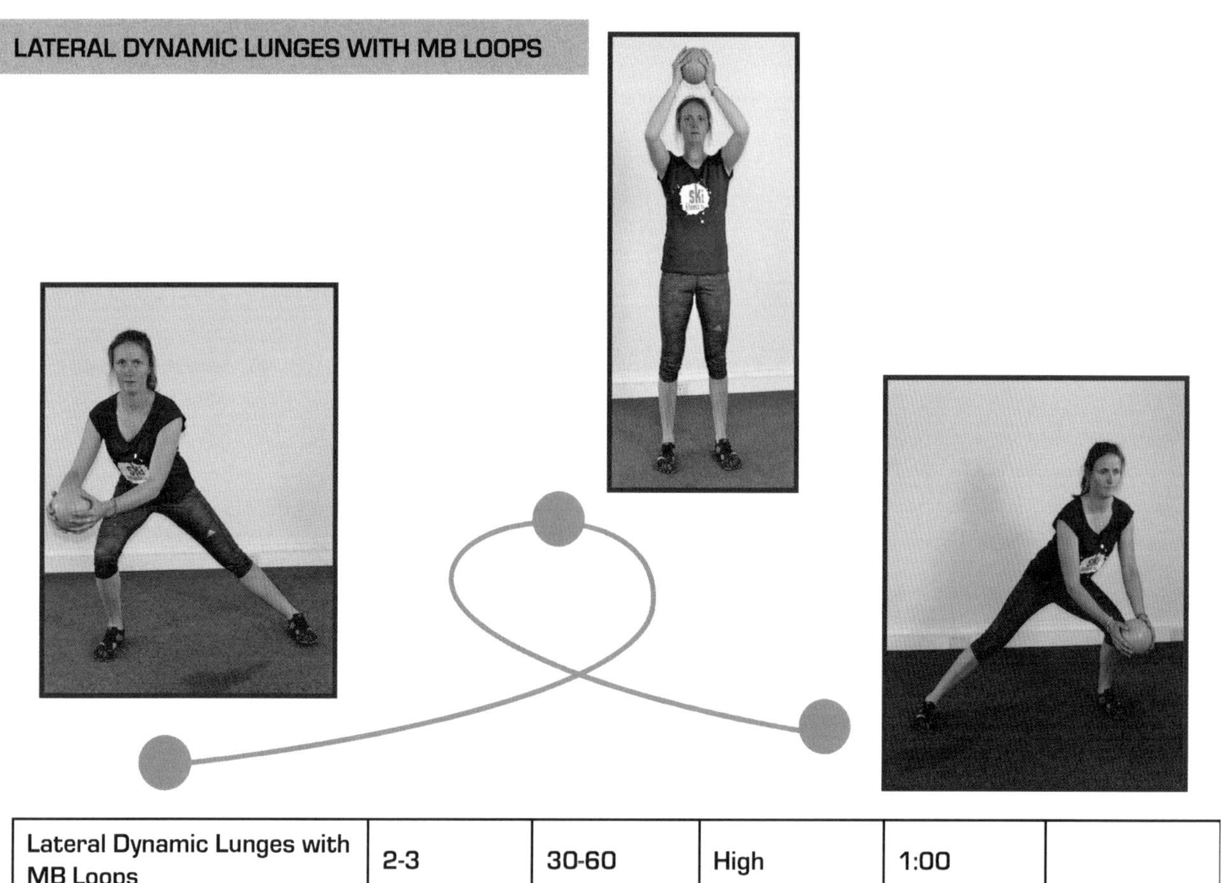

Lateral Dynamic Lunges with MB Loops	2-3	30-60	High	1:00	

Why: Exercises the frontal (side-to-side) plane, and improves single leg strength, with moving core and shoulders.

How: Start in a side lunge, with your weight (70%) over a bent leg (knee 90 degrees), body and foot facing forward with your knee in line with your second toe. Your unweighted (30%) leg should be nearly straight with only a slight bend at the knee. Keep a neutral spine. Hold the MB in your hands just the other side of your weighted knee. Power-off the weighted leg, stepping so your feet are together, then lunge to the other side with your other foot. At the same time, your hands and the medicine ball should 'loop-the-loop' (under-over) across your body to the far side of the newly weighted (70%) leg. Repeat the other way back to the starting position.

Start slowly for technique and build up the speed once you are confident of perfect technique.

Progressions: BOSUs on far weighted legs or BOSU in the middle.

Outdoor alternative: Rock/log instead of MB.

KNEELING/STANDING ON STABILITY BALL

Kneeling/Standing on Stability Ball					Fun

Why: This works on your balance and as you progress this will enable you to complete or improve some of the other exercises on the ball. Practice followed by rest will help create new 'neural pathways' (brain connections) to enable you to improve and progress – so keep working at it.

How: Kneeling with your feet on the ground, form a square on the front of a ball with your knees and hands, then roll forward slowly with your feet coming off the floor. This gentle rolling technique is easier than trying to 'climb' onto the ball. No given reps or sets – just play around.

Progressions: Hands and knees; just knees; hold MB; play 'catch'; one knee/one arm and alternate; standing; squats; weights; jump on the ball.

Outdoor alternative: Balance on fallen trees.

P5 PHASE 5 CIRCUIT TRAINING

Circuits are characterised by moving from one exercise to another with no rest times, and entail completing the full circuit of different (and complementary) exercises, resting and then completing the circuit again. Exercises in circuits, as in this case, are often for a length of time (e.g. 30 seconds) rather than a number of repetitions.

Circuits convert strength into power and endurance, which is just what you need for skiing: strong muscles that are able to perform bursts of high intensity, repeatedly. Think about how you ski, i.e. how long a pitch of skiing do you do before you stop? Then play around with duration and rest time:

No rest between circuit exercises
Rest 4 minutes at end of each circuit and repeat 3 to 5 times.

MODERATE

- Start off each exercise for 30 seconds, then try 45 secs and 60 secs

HARD

- Start 60 secs, then try 90 secs and 120 secs

P5C1 PHASE 5 CIRCUIT 1

P5C1.1 BOSU JUMPS/CIRCUIT

Why: These are plyometric exercises to improve the strength in your legs.

How: Jump up and down on a BOSU (dome up to start with).

Progressions: Jump on and off BOSU; jump from BOSU to BOSU (two or more); add benches, wobble boards, steps etc., to make a circuit.

P5C1.2 LATERAL HOPS/SKATERS

Why: One-legged plyometrics with weight transfer from side-to-side are very relevant for skiing.

How: Jump laterally from one leg to another. Mark a set distance that you can just achieve.

Progressions: Add a BOSU or two; widen the distance.

P5C1.3 DB TURKISH GET UP

Why: For when you fall over! But, it is also great total bodywork for skiing.

How: Lie on your back on the floor with a dumbbell in one hand at arms length above your shoulder. Activate your core, tuck one leg (opposite to DB arm side) under the other leg, sit up whilst holding the dumbbell overhead. From the sitting position, place your foot (same side as DB arm) on the floor and stand up, keeping your arm straight and a strong core. You can use your hand to help this movement. Reverse the movements lowering under control, then repeat.
Change sides half way through the time.

Progressions: Increase DB weight; same side arm and leg; make movement more dynamic (faster).

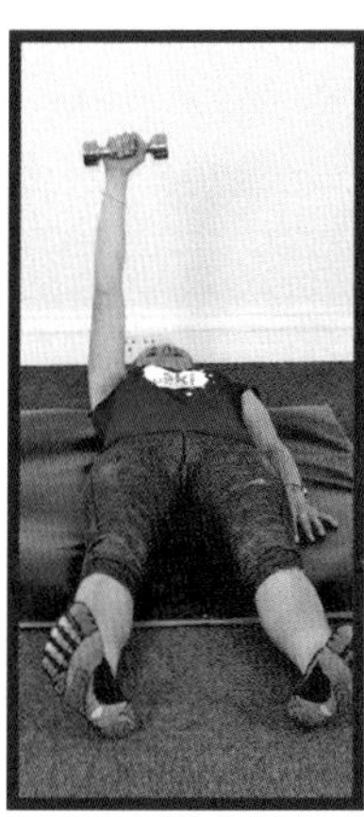

P5C1.4 SKIING JACKKNIFE

Why: Builds core stability with lower leg moving side-to-side.

How: Place your hands in a press-up position on the floor with your feet/shins on a stability ball. Draw your knees to your chest, bring the ball in and twist your lower body to one side so your knees are pointing out to one side. Extend your legs to return to start position keeping the ball in control at all times. Keep your core strong and your back neutral. Repeat, this time with knees going to the other side. Repeat alternating sides.

Progressions: One leg; hands on BOSU or similar.

P5C1.5 SB LEG CURLS

Why: Strengthens hamstrings.

How: Lie on your back on the floor with your feet/heels on a stability ball. Lift your hips into a straight 'bridge' position. Start the exercise by bending (flexing) both legs at the knee so the ball comes towards your body. The soles of your feet go on top of the ball and your hips and body push upwards. There should be a straight line from your knees, through hips to your shoulders. Return to the bridge position and repeat.

Progressions: One leg; weight on hips.

P5C1.6 RUSSIAN TWISTS

With MB

Why: This exercise is a dynamic twist pattern.

How: Place your feet on the floor, and your head and shoulders on a Swiss ball, with your arms straight up and your hands together over the centre of your chest. Keep your tongue in roof of your mouth to stabilise the neck muscles. Keeping your hips up and as level as possible, twist your upper body to one side a full 90 degrees so your arms point sideways. The ball should move underneath you, with one shoulder on the ball, one directly above the other. Your arms should stay straight with your hands staying directly in line with your chest. Move your head in line with your arms. If you fall off, well done for trying! It's not far to fall, so try again, focusing on getting the ball to move so you stay directly above it. Return to the starting position and go to other side.

Progressions: Medicine ball/weight in hands; make the movement more dynamic; keep the head pointing upwards (not moving with hands).

P5C1.7 BENCH LOWER ABS

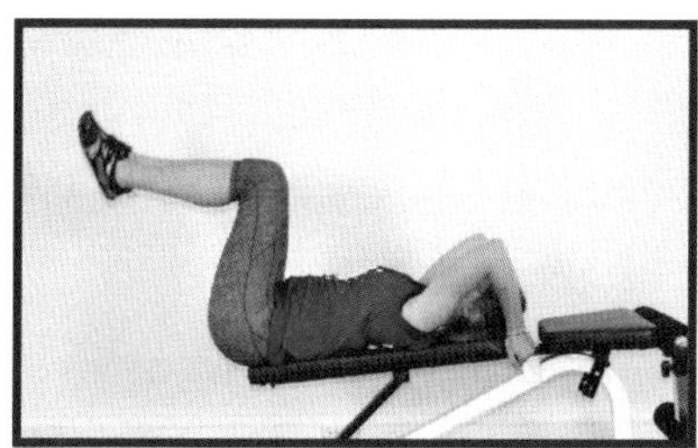

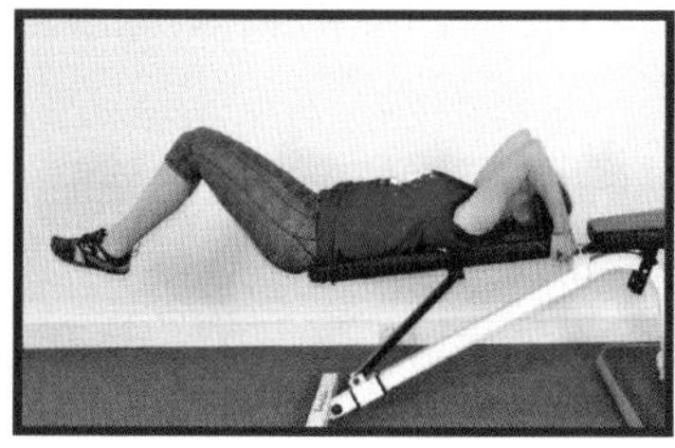

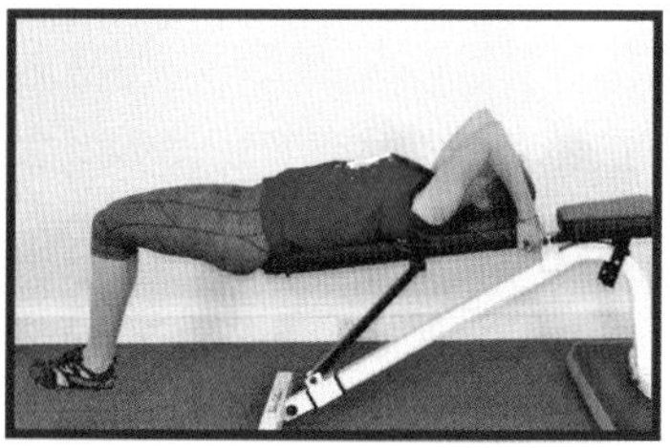

Why: This exercise facilitates lower abdominal work in semi-supported position.

How: Lie on your back on a bench (possibly raising the 'head end' of the bench on a small step). Bring your knees up so your hips and knees are both at 90 degrees. Keep your tongue in the roof of your mouth. Lower your legs to nearly touch the floor from your hips, keeping 90 degrees at the knee and return to the start position. Do not go past 90 degrees with the hips on the return as it will use the wrong muscles (hip flexors).

Progressions: Incorporate a slight vertical lift of the hips/knees when you return to 90 degrees.

P5C1.8 SINGLE LEG BOSU BALANCE

Why: Improves single leg stability.

How: Stand on one leg on the centre of a BOSU (dome up) and balance.
Use your other leg to gently touch the BOSU if needed, initially to help stabilise.

Progressions: Hand reaches; shin/toe touches with hand; dome down.

P5C2 PHASE 5 CIRCUIT 2

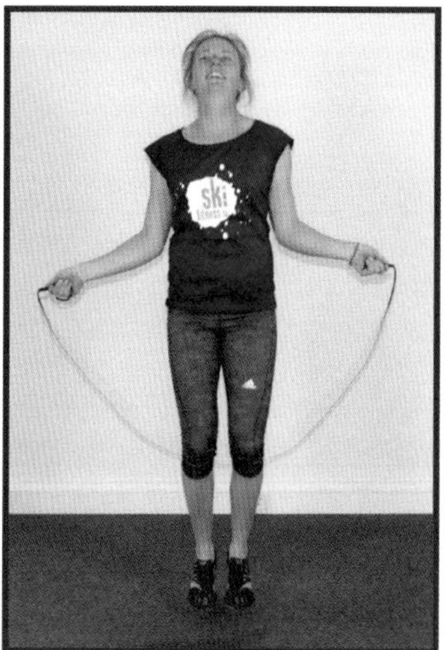

P5C2.1 SKIPPING

Why: This is a plyometric exercise to strengthen your legs and improve coordination and balance.

How: Choose a normal skipping rope or a speed rope, which is a plastic rope that is quicker through the air. Remember the school playground and off you go!

Progressions: Single leg.

P5C2.2 SB PRONE LATERAL ROLL - LEGS

Why: Great core exercise contrasting the forces of stability and movement. Works on balance and twist pattern.

How: Place your feet/legs on the stability ball, and your hands on the ground in a facing down (prone) position. Keep your hips up and neutral spine throughout. Twist your hips/legs side-to-side. Start off with only small movements.

Progressions: A ball can be placed on the knees, shins, feet or toes getting progressively harder. Increase ovement (side-to-side, distance) and speed of movement.

P5C2.3 SB SUPINE BRIDGE LEG LIFTS

Why: Works the back in connection with the glutes, legs and shoulders. It also works frontal plane (side-to-side) movement, which is often overlooked in many gym programmes, and is very important for skiing. It works the contrasting forces of stability and movement.

How: Start with a bridge position facing upwards (supine) with your head and shoulders on the ball, and your feet shoulder-width apart on the floor, your knees directly above your feet. Keep your arms straight out sideways. Offset by moving your body to the right with your right shoulder just coming off the ball support, then lift your left leg, off the floor, by extending at the knee. Keep your hips up and level, with your knees in line. Hold for three seconds and then return your foot to floor, move body back into the middle of the ball and repeat moving left this time and lifting your right leg.

Progressions: You can go further out, hold for longer, with your supporting foot on a stability disc.

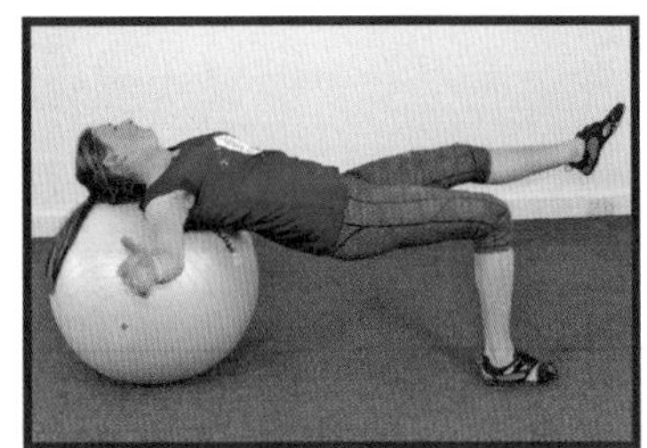

P5C2.4 LATERAL LUNGE MB LOOP-THE-LOOP

See exercise as detailed on Page 65

P5C2.5 SB PRONE LATERAL BALL ROLLS – ARMS

Why: Core stability, twist and frontal movement pattern plus balance.

How: Place your feet on floor with arms 'cuddling' a stability ball. Start with your feet stationary and move your upper body and the ball side-to-side. Start slowly with small movements and build up speed and distance of movement. This exercise is quite subtle. Try not to lose balance, but push further each time and gradually build up speed. Progress to fast, side-to-side movement with dynamic recoil and with your far foot coming off the floor.

Progressions: Partner wrestle.

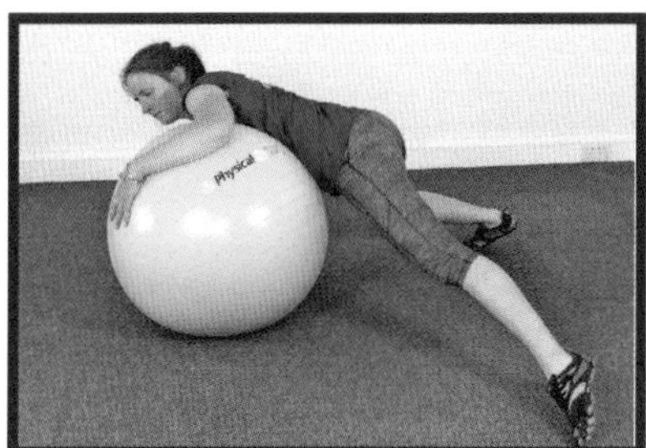

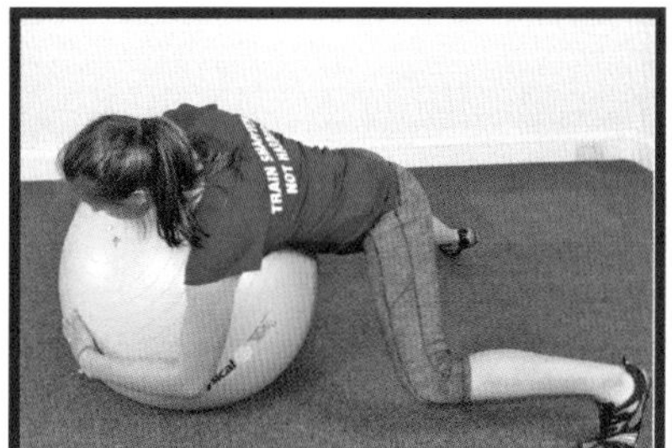

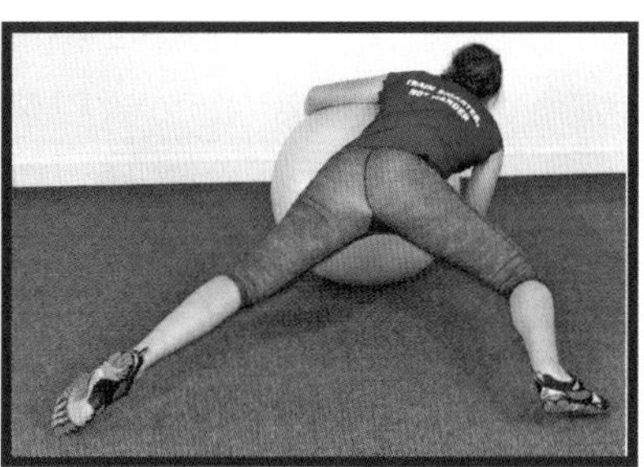

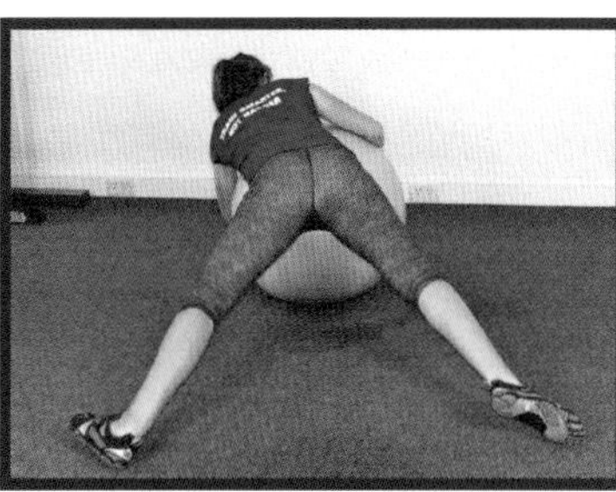

P5C2.6 SB PRESS-UP & JACKKNIFE

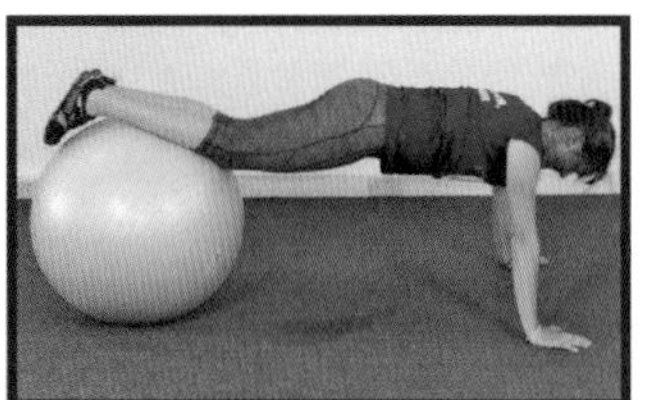

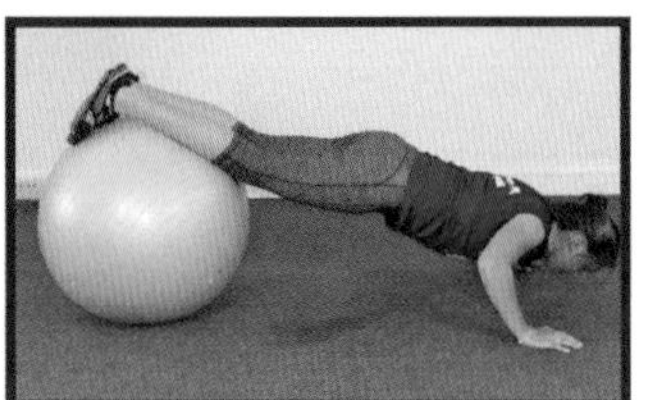

Progression: jackknife and press at same time

Why: Core connection of upper and low body. Improves chest, arm, core and shoulder strength via the press-up. Improves lower abdominal strength and coordination via the jackknife.

How: Place your hands on the floor and feet on the stability ball. Draw your knees into your chest bringing the ball with you and return (jackknife) then put your chest to the floor and return (press-up). Repeat both actions.

Progressions: Press at same time as jackknife; ski jackknives (side-to-side movement).

P5C2.7 BOSU SQUAT ISOMETRIC HOLD

Why: Improves isometric (non-moving) strength and balance. Replicates a 'schuss' (ski tuck) or long ski run without too much leg movement.

How: Stand on BOSU and squat into a tuck position. Keep your spin neutral and then just hold/balance in that position without moving.

Progressions: Eyes closed; stand on a stability ball instead of BOSU.

P6S1 PHASE 6 SESSION 1

PLYOMETRIC SESSION

Before starting these exercises, please read Chapter 4 on plyometric training.

Warm-up properly making sure any tight muscles are really warm. If you are very tight, consider postponing the session. A 50% intensity of each exercise is generally the best warm-up. Do not static stretch as it will reduce plyometric recoil.

Incorporate a four-day recovery time.

P6S1.1 BOX JUMPS

60 secs each set
3 minutes rest between sets
4 sets
4 mins rest before next exercise

Why: This is as close as you can get to dynamic skiing in a controlled environment, which means it is good for rehabilitation as well as for those who want to get fit for the slopes at home.

Progressions

How: Use a plyometric box or a step from a step class. On both you can adjust the height, which will be your intensity, so start low and increase accordingly. Jump two footed on and off the box/step.

Progressions: Jump forward off the box and then jump backward back onto the box; do it sideways; do a mixture of all angles: front, back, side, diagonal. Use different boxes and make a circuit, jumping between them and varying sequences, e.g. BOSUs, benches, boxes, steps etc.

Outdoor alternative: Tractor tyres, steps, logs etc.

P6S1.2 LATERAL JUMPS TWO-FOOTED

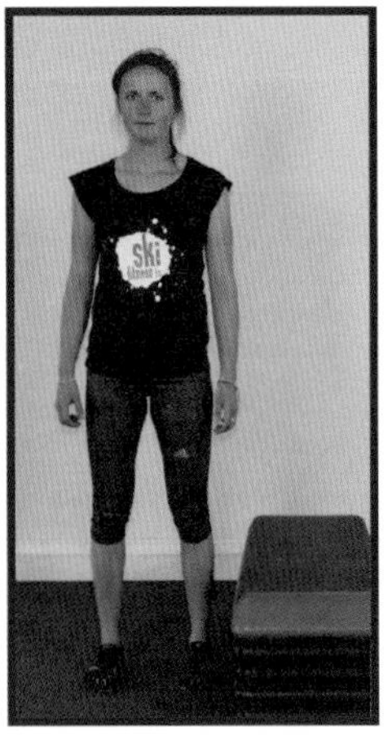

30 secs each set
90 secs rest between sets
4 sets
4 mins rest before next exercise

Why: Works on frontal plane weight transfer, keeping a still upper body with strong dynamic core.

How: Choose a set distance such as over a mat or a box, then jump two-footed side to side. Keep the quality of balance and precision throughout thirty seconds.

Progressions: Change what you jump over, varying the height and jump distance.

Outdoor: Jump over logs, tractor tyres, etc. Anything goes!

P6S1.3 ONE-FOOTED JUMPS

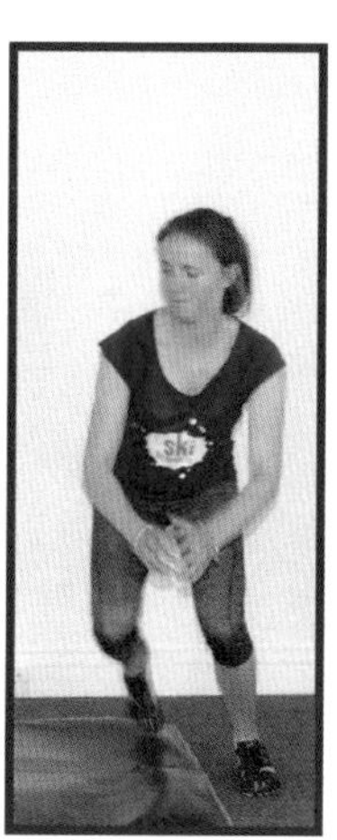

30-60 secs each set
3 minutes rest between sets
4 sets

Why: Works on one-legged frontal plane weight transfer, keeping a still upper body with strong dynamic core.

How: Choose a distance that is possible for you to jump sideways and land on one leg but a distance that is also challenging. Go for distance rather than height. You can use a gym mat, tape on the floor or sticks. Engage your core, power off one leg sideways and land on the other leg. Power off that leg returning to the start position. Keep your core strong, spine neutral and knees aligned with your second toe (as always!).

Progressions: Widen the distance; faster movements; use the timings above as a starting point then vary.

Outdoor: This exercise is best performed outdoors.

P6S2 PHASE 6 SESSION 2

DYNAMIC STRENGTH

This is more of an outdoor play session than an actual programme (completing the cycle, Phases 1 to 6). One of the key elements is the fun:risk ratio. Remember, it is only fun until you get hurt. Increased risk increases your neural connections and fully recruits all of the necessary muscles, because your body is anticipating and reacting to the stress, fear and potentially painful situation you are initiating. However, by adding such risk in a controlled environment, as in a training session, you are able to increase or decrease the risk depending on variables such as tiredness, complexity, injury potential, etc.

"Create safe emergencies"

This belongs to the philosophy of 'train hard, ski easy'. If you have trained yourself for something much harder than you actually experience, you will have more fun. There will also be a reduced risk of injury.

The Irony of Risk - lack of exposure to risk, especially in a controlled and progressive environment, actually increases your risk of injury and death.

P6S2.1 JUMP ON SB

Why: It's fun and potentially painful if got wrong – which means it will fully activate your nervous system. It is similar to having to push your body to complete a crucial jump-turn in a narrow couloir.

Warning: This is potentially very dangerous for an untrained individual and is obviously undertaken at your own risk.

How: Make sure you have learned how to stand on a stability ball first. Jump two footed from the ground onto a stability ball. Have a lot of space around you and soft landing. Practice on a BOSU (both sides).

Progressions: Jump onto other objects.

P6S2.2 COOLBOARD OFFSET SQUATS

Why: Improves strength and balance.

How: Learn to stand on coolboard with maybe the support of a bar. Once you can balance, start to play around, moving the board laterally, then try some squats in the middle, and also try squats offset to each side. Play with squatting one side then the other, then try alternating sides on each squat.

Progressions: Eyes closed - whiteout conditions!

P6S2.3 TREE CLIMB

Why: Improves strength and coordination. Useful for pull-ups and body rows.

How: Find a tree and have a play. Try pull-ups with different hand grips. When you get tired, bring your legs up onto a branch and try some body rows.

Progressions: One-arm pulls.

P6S2.4 SINGLE LEG HOPS (STEPPING STONES)

Why: This is a single leg plyometric exercise, but with increased risk to fully engage neural pathways and ensure strong/intelligent muscles not strong/stupid muscles.

How: Find some posts, logs, stepping stones. Hop from one to the other.

Progressions: Increase difficulty/risk.

P6S2.5 SLACKLINING

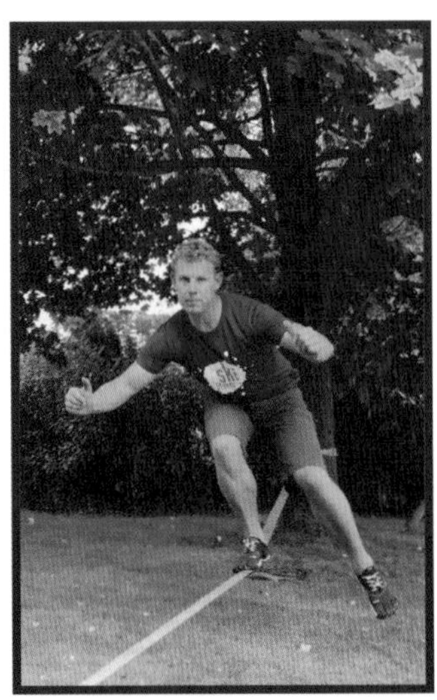

Why: Improves strength, balance and concentration, and is fun, mindful and addictive...

How: Put up a slackline between two trees and start to play. You can use ski poles to start with. Having a shorter and tighter line is easier. Hold your arms up and make very small adjustments with your arms to help you balance. Sink your weight into the line, slightly sitting into it. Rest overnight (or for a couple of days) and your body will rewire networks to help you progress (neurogenesis).

Progressions: Look online for inspiration.

P6S2.6 LOWER ABS SB

Why: Having a still upper body and dynamic lower body is a great core exercise for skiing.

How: Position the small of your back on a stability ball, bring your legs up with your knees at 90 degrees, and with your hands, hold an anchor of some description (bench, cable machine) to stabilise your position. (It might take a couple of attempts to find the correct position.) Keep your head level and your tongue in the roof of your mouth to stabilise your neck. Lower your legs from the hip, keeping knees at 90 degrees, until your toes nearly touch the floor and then return your legs to the start position.

Progressions: Vary speed and then the angle of your legs.

P6S2.7 WASHING MACHINE

As detailed on Page 64

P6S2.8 ROPE CLIMB

Why: Improves upper body strength.

How: Tie a rope to a tree and climb up and down it.

Progressions: Don't use your legs.

RECOVERY CIRCUITS

Training is not about how hard you train, it is about how well you 'bounce back' and recover from the training stress on the body. Along with proper nutrition and high quality sleep, recovery exercises can enhance and speed-up recovery (see Chapter 4.C).

Benefits

- Puts the body into 'parasympathetic nervous system' mode, which is a recovery mode (rest/repair instead of fight/flight).
- The movement helps pump blood back to the heart (vasoconstriction) easing pressure on the heart.
- Sends blood, oxygen and energy to chosen (moving) muscles.
- Utilises and trains the complete range of the lungs.
- Stretches tight muscles.
- Builds energy.
- Mental relaxation.

This is achieved by building energy as opposed to depleting energy. To ensure you stay in the 'building' rather than 'depleting' phase, you need to keep the intensity at a low level.

Intensity guide:

- You should be able to complete these exercises after a meal.
- You should not get out of breath at any stage.
- You should be able to breathe through your nose throughout.

The most important thing is diaphragmatic breathing.

DIAPHRAGMATIC BREATHING

BELLY/NOSE BREATHING

Optimal breathing is breathing in through your nose with your belly coming out, then breathing out (through your mouth or nose) with your belly coming in.

Most people have an inverted breathing pattern, i.e. their belly coming in when they breathe in.

Tip: Watch a baby breathe – they do it right instinctively.

Exercises:
Standing-up, put a hand on your chest and a hand on your belly. Breathe in through your nose making sure only your hand on your belly moves for the first two thirds of your in-breath. Your chest hand should only move/rise during the last third of your in-breath. As you breathe out (through mouth or nose), reverse the process making sure your belly hand moves in. Exhale completely. When you've finished exhaling, try just exhaling a little bit more. This will ensure a full exchange of air in your lungs. Some people really struggle with this, so continue to practice and practice and it will get easier and more automatic.

If you are having trouble doing this exercise standing up, try lying down and use a visual reference such as a block or water bottle on your belly. As you breathe in through your nose the object should rise and as you breathe out the object should lower.

RC1 RECOVERY CIRCUIT 1

Always breathe in through nose. You can breathe out through mouth or nose. The slower the better. If you cannot keep your breath control, stop.

About 10 reps or 1 minute on each exercise – no need to be precise on timings in the Recovery Programme.

RC1.1 BREATHING SQUATS

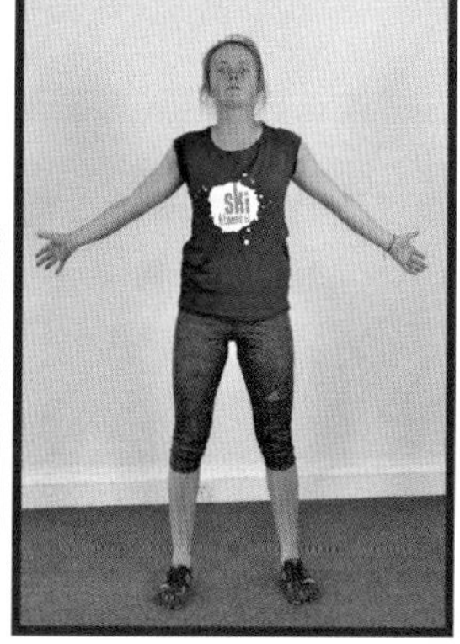

These are great exercises that can be used for movement snacks as well as recovery – they help with digestion, blood sugar balance, elimination, vasoconstriction (blood pumping) and more! Stand with your feet shoulder-width apart, squat down as low as you can go, pain free and without getting out of breath. Breathe out as you squat down, breathe in through your nose as you come up.

RC1.2 PELVIC TILTS

This exercise can be performed standing, lying down or sitting on a stability ball. Tilt your pelvis forward very slowly to the end range of your movement as you are breathing in. To tip the pelvis the right way, for a forward tip, think of the pelvis as bowl of water and you are pouring the water out the front of the bowl. Then tilt your pelvis backwards breathing out. There is a knack to getting this right, take your time and practise. If your knees and shoulders are moving, you haven't got it quite right yet. You can progress to sideways movements and circles in both directions.

Neutral pelvis

Forward pelvis /

*Backward pelvis *

Hip hike

Hip hike

RC1.3 HORSE STANCE DYNAMIC

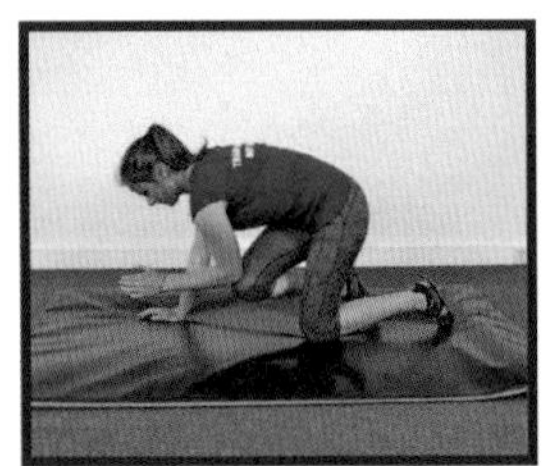

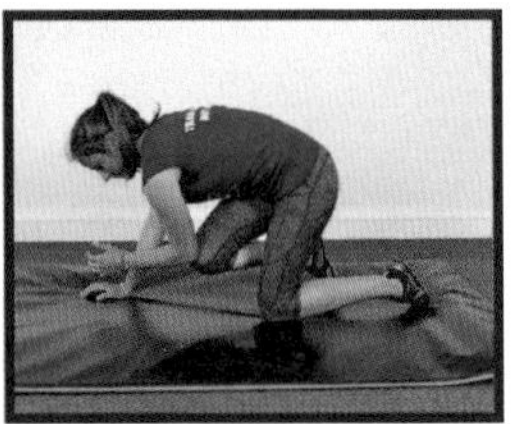

Kneel on the floor (a mat is kind to the knees) in a 'horse-stance' with your shoulders over your hands and your hips shoulder-width apart over your knees. Bring your opposite elbow to opposite knee, touching if you can, breathing out. Then move your leg and arm up as high as you can, breathing in. Your arm should be at 45 degrees with your thumb pointed up. Repeat on the same side for around 30 seconds and then swap sides.

RC1.4 PRONE COBRAS

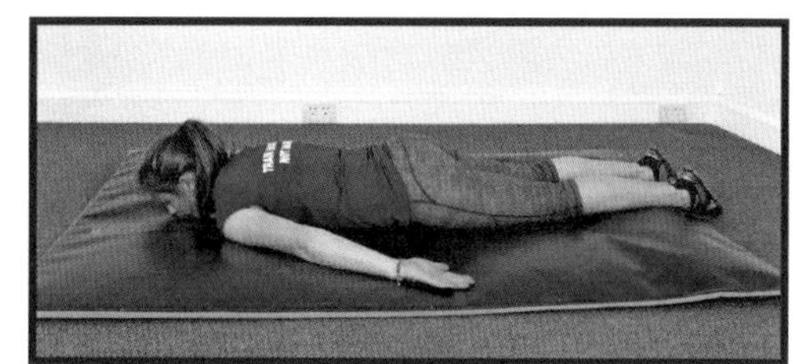

Lie face down on a mat (prone) with your arms by your side, palms up. Breathing in, lift up your head and upper body and rotate your arms outwards so your thumbs face up. Imagine you are holding two cups of water at the top of the movement. Keep your chin tucked in throughout the movement. Exhale and return to the start position. If your lower back hurts do not go as high and/or activate your glutes.

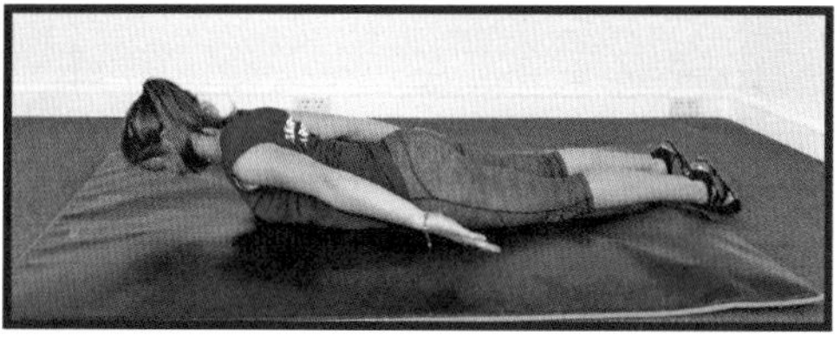

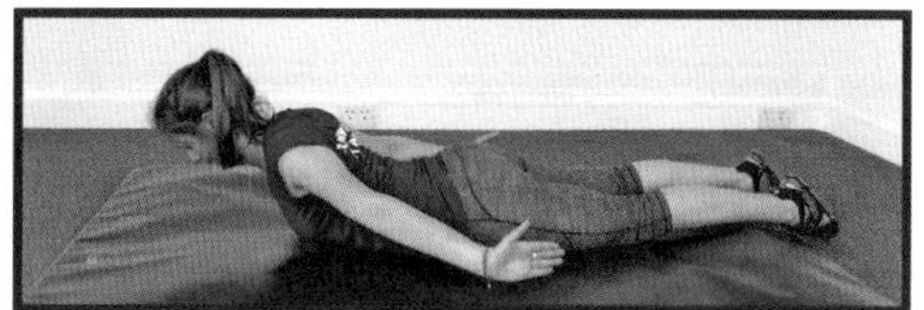

RC1.5 NECK ROTATIONS

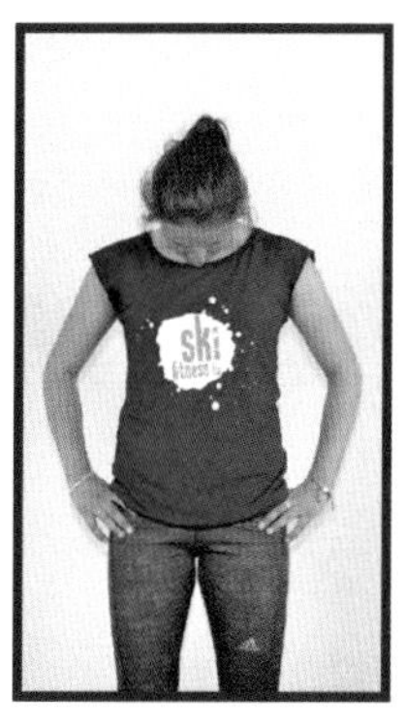

Do not perform full circles if you have neck problems or you feel dizzy. Imagine you are moving your nose around a clock face. Breathe in as you go up and round; breathe out as you go down and round. Change direction halfway through your allocated time for this exercise.

RC1.6 CROSS CRAWL

This is one of my favourite exercises as it balances both sides of the brain. If you have problems coordinating this one, keep trying because it will really help you. From a standing position put your arms in the air, out to your sides with a bend at the elbow. Lifting a leg bring opposite elbow to the knee, breathing out. Return to start position breathing in and repeat on the other side (so alternating sides). Remember the slower you complete these movements the better.

RC2 RECOVERY CIRCUIT 2

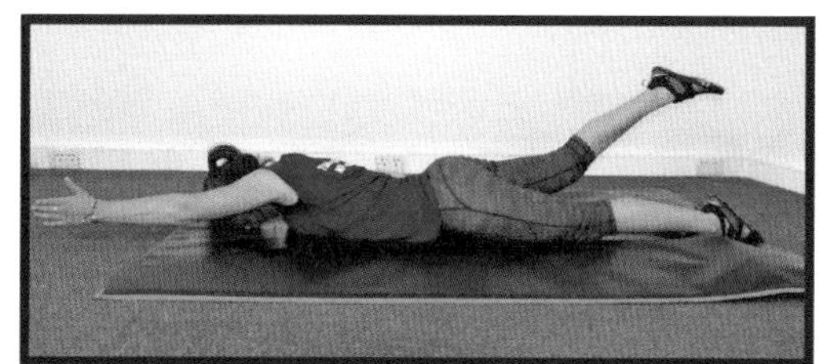

RC2.1 SUPERMAN

Lie face down. Lift your opposite arm and leg off the floor, breathing in. Your arm should be 45 degrees with thumb pointed up. Return your leg and arm to the floor, breathing out. Alternate sides.

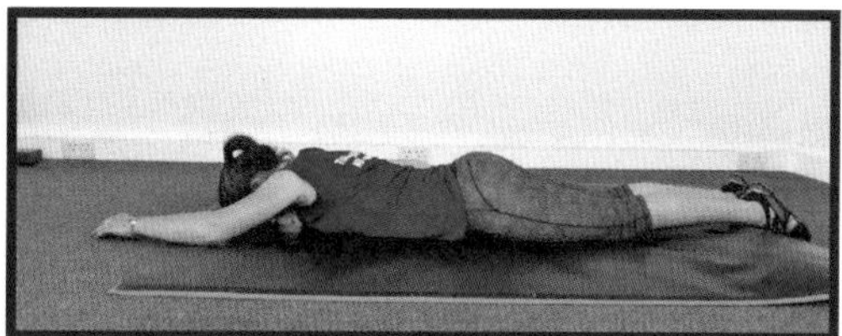

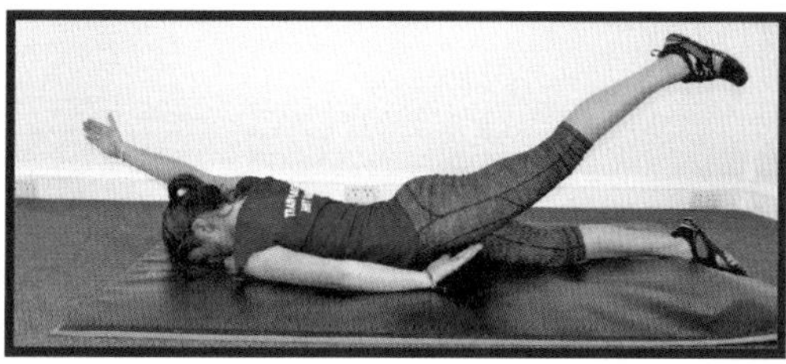

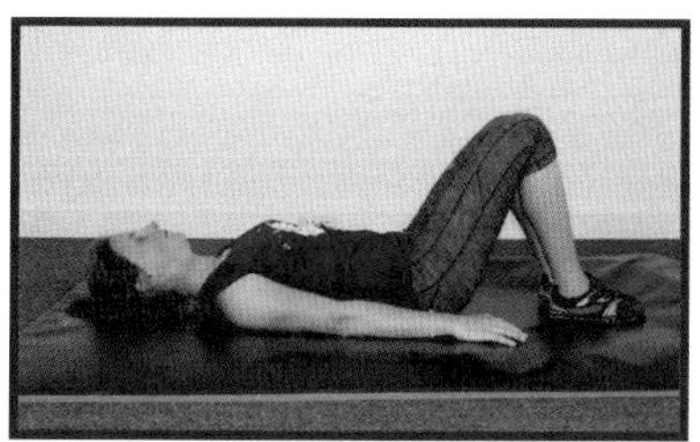

RC2.2 LEG TUCK

Lie on your back with your legs bent. Bring your knees into your chest and hold onto your legs, breathing out. Return to start position breathing in.

RC2.3 WOODCHOP

Stand upright with both arms in the air. From the hip, bend down with both arms going to the floor on one side, breathing out. Keep only a slight bend at the knee. Return to start position breathing in, possibly going further back, arching the back. Then repeat, going down to other side of the body.

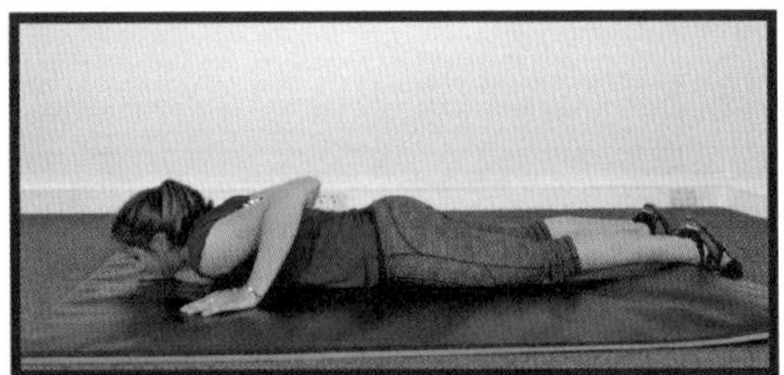

RC2.4 MCKENZIE PRESS-UP

Lie face down on the ground with hands in a push-up position. Push yourself up, keeping your pelvis on the ground, breathing out. Return to floor breathing in.

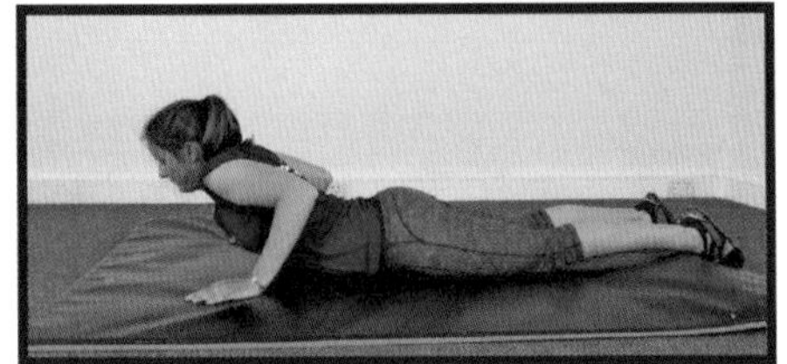

RC2.5 THORACIC MOBILISATIONS

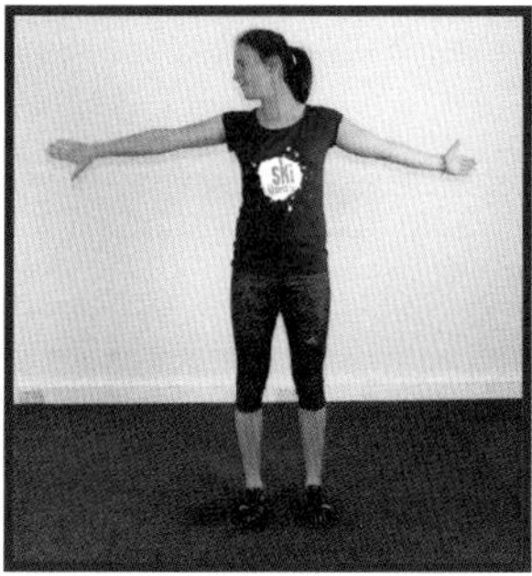

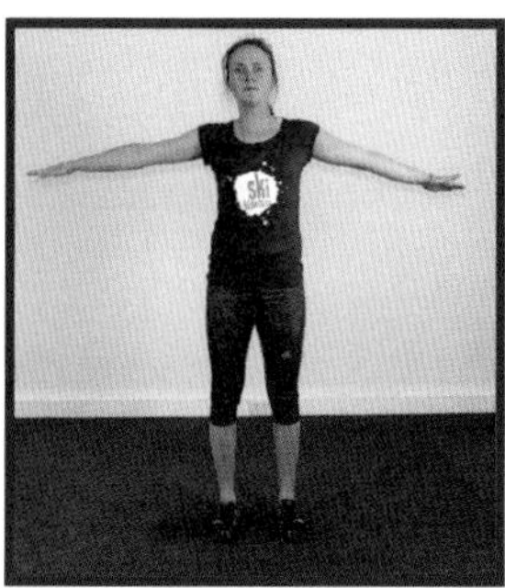

From a standing position or lying vertically on a foam roller, hold your arms out straight to the side. Have one thumb pointing up and one thumb pointing down. Look at the thumb pointing down and rotate your head and your hands so that you are now looking at the other hand which is now pointing down (with your other hand now pointing up). Repeat moving both head and hands returning to the starting point. You can breathe in one way, breathe out the other, it doesn't matter which.

RC2.6 ALTERNATE NOSTRIL BREATHING

Hold your finger closing one nostril and breathe in through the other one. Change hands, close off the other nostril and breathe out. Breathe back in through same nostril then change hands blocking off this nostril and breathe out and back in through the other one. Repeat.

This section gives you the rationale and the information to complete the programme effectively.

Sports massage is also recommended.

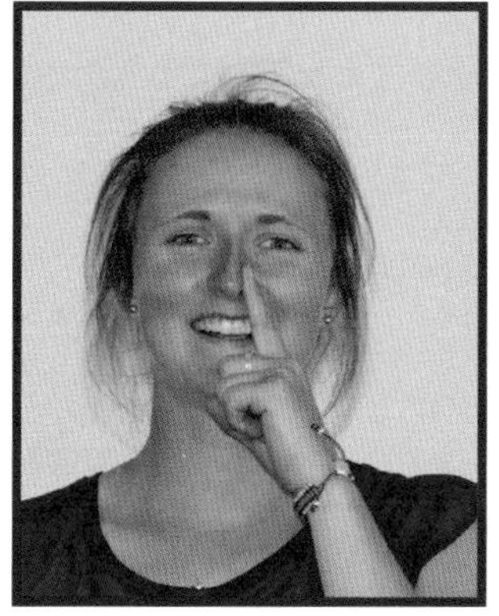

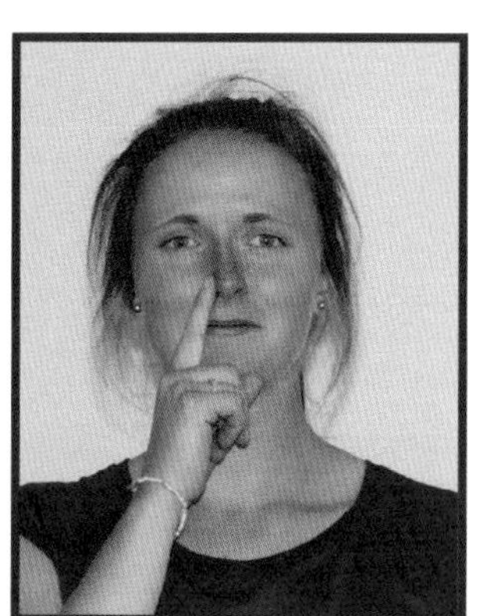

CHAPTER 4

SUCCESS INFO

A) STIMULUS: RESPONSE

Training is all about recovery.

You do not get the benefits of training from the training. You get the benefits of training from the recovery afterwards.

Training is simply a stimulus for the body to respond to. Training actually breaks down the muscle, injuring and micro-tearing the muscle fibres. The intensity you train at and the current state your body is in determines how much 'muscle tearing' and injury there is. This is a stimulus for your body to allocate resources to repair the injured muscle back to where it started. Furthermore, the body knows that if you do something once, you will probably do it again, so it sends extra energy to not only repair the body back to 'normal' but, to make it fitter and stronger and so perform better the next time it is needed. This is called Supercompensation.

Supercompensation: The reason for training – to recover to a state where you perform better than you did before training.

Training Variables:
Starting point – the state your body is in: includes posture, stage in training programme, core support.
Training – load, intensity, density, technique.
Rest – quality and length/time.

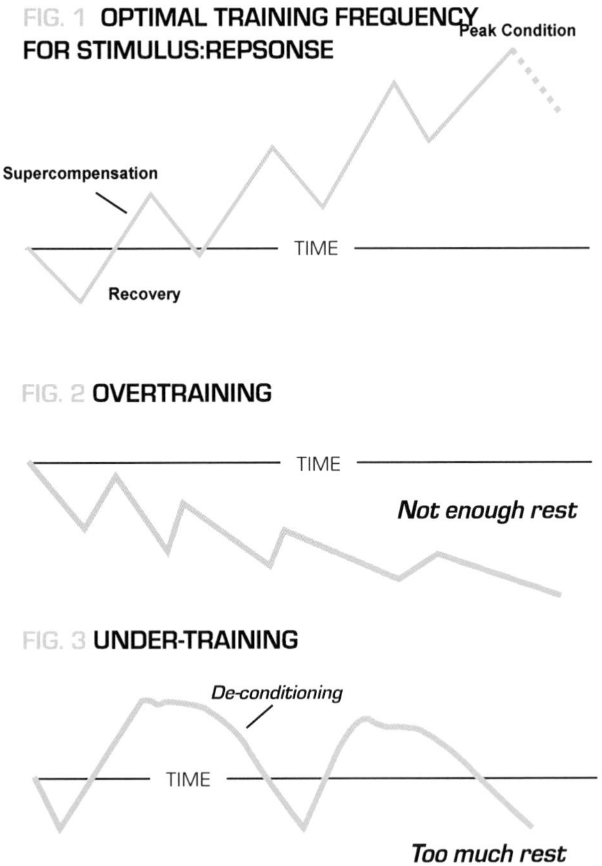

Overtraining signs:
Elevated heart rate
Muscle soreness
Depression
Change in personality
Anger
Insomnia
Lethargy
Insatiable thirst
Illness – immune system compromised
Injury
Difficulty concentrating
Lack of motivation
Not progressing in training programme
Reduced performance

Overtraining Assessment

Pulse test: take your pulse (resting heart rate) each morning at the same time.

Measurement: find your pulse, time 15 seconds and count your beats, starting with zero, then times your number of beats by four to get your beats per minute (BPM).

Assessment: Identify an average and if it is elevated on any one morning by say, ten beats or more, you need to rest.

DOMS – Delayed Onset of Muscle Soreness
The longer it takes the worse it is! If you have very painful muscles the day after exercise, count yourself lucky as it is far worse to have the pain two days after exercise as the longer the delay, the more damage you have done. But, do not worry, just rest longer and better. DOMS is normal and generally occurs when you change your programme, or do something different that your body is not used to. This is why we change, periodise and cross-train, to make sure your body can handle anything the mountain throws at it.

TAPERING

Tapering is making sure your body gets to the start line in peak condition. Generally, this involves reducing or 'tapering' down your training load and intensity a couple of weeks before your ski holiday. This ensures you are fully recovered when you start your event or holiday. Obviously, too much tapering will result in de-conditioning (a reduction in performance). The balance between too little and not enough tapering time is personal and dependent on your training variables (starting point, training and rest). Practice/experience, monitoring and 'knowing your body' help you decide on your own tapering length of time. Two weeks is a good guideline timeframe, i.e. start reducing your training load two weeks before your first day skiing.

Around 80% of those lining up at the London Marathon start are injured, over-trained and just plain tired.

Daily Exercise Readiness Questionnaire

Morning Pulse: .... Beats above/below average ....

Perception:

Energy levels on 1-10 scale (1=low 10=high): ....

Muscle soreness on 1-10 scale (1=low 10=high): ....

Stress level on 1-10 scale (1=low 10=high): ....

Mood on 1-10 scale (1 = grumpy 10 = jumping for joy) ....

Hours of Sleep: .... Restless/sound ....

Download a copy at www.skifitness.tv

B) TRAINING

There is no point in lifting light weights, but if it hurts, you're doing it incorrectly.

TRAINING INTENSITY

Intensity vs Density
Lifting weights in the gym at 10 reps progressing to 1 Repetition Maximum (the maximum weight you can lift once) is 'intense' exercise. Going to a circuit class, Zumba class, or step class is a 'high density' exercise because a large volume of exercise is completed in a relatively short period of time. In general, too much exposure to 'high intensity' lifting commonly leads to connective tissue injuries, such as joint capsule strains, ligament strain, and connective tissue strain. Too much 'density' (volume of weight lifting usually at 10 RM – 30 RM or aerobic intensities) of exercise most commonly causes muscular challenges, such as painful trigger points, soreness from waste accumulation, muscle imbalances, and progressively slower recovery times between workouts.

For ski conditioning we want to focus on intensity, only focusing on density in the power/endurance phase (Phase 5).

TECHNIQUE, TECHNIQUE, TECHNIQUE

Technique is everything when it comes to weight training. Yes, you want to 'work to failure', you want high intensity, but not at the cost of technique. Working to failure, is working to your maximum: it is failure when you cannot lift anymore, or cannot perform or complete any more repetitions of that exercise at that weight. Most people, when trying to do this, go beyond failure of technique and carry on performing the exercise very badly, recruiting fresh muscles that would not ideally be used in this movement pattern, creating a cascade of problems.

Fitness is so specific: if you train doing pull-ups on a 2 inch diameter bar you can't do as many pull-ups on a 1 inch diameter bar. The SAID (Specific Adaptation to Imposed Demand) principle states 'You get what you train for'. So, if you train with poor technique, you will training the wrong muscles and doing more harm than good. For example, if you squat with poor alignment of the spine you will be encouraging and amplifying this misalignment every time you load the spine in a squat movement pattern in everyday life and when skiing. This will lead to reduced performance, pain and injury.

Another example: with plyometrics, make sure you rest properly, otherwise you will train yourself to be weak and slow – the opposite of what you were training for.

If your core is fatigued, you will train yourself to perform movements without optimal support = poor technique = poor performance and injury.

- use repetition reserve (see below)
- work to failure of technique, not failure of being able to do the movement

POSTURE

The body has an optimal posture, which it moves around and returns to for optimal performance. This includes:

- natural curves in your upper and lower back/spine (S-shape)
- correct length/tension relationship of muscles (flexibility), especially antagonistic (opposite) ones.

It is not that you should always be in this perfect posture, it is more that you should move each way, equally around this position, always returning to the optimal. Most people's posture is compromised by too much sitting, unbalanced training, repetitive movement patterns in sport and work, poor diet, injury, emotional issues ... I could go on!
When moving, optimal posture gives you the optimal axis of rotation around your body's joints. You want this because without it you will never reach your full potential and ultimately, you will injure the joint or refer injury to another part of the body. In fact this point is really important as most injury or pain is 'referred' or 'caused' by a problem somewhere else. Always be careful about treating symptoms: you need to find the cause of the problem for long-lasting results.

Lower Back Pain (LBP) Scenario:

- Generally caused by too much curve in the upper back.
- Caused by too much sitting.
- When you come to your training (or gardening/ DIY etc.) you take the curve out of your upper back to complete the task, but in doing so you put too much curve in your lower back.
- This causes 'pinch points' which, if your core strength (tummy muscles) is less than optimal, will not be able to support.
- So you end up with lower back pain that you treat with all manner of solutions but all you really needed to do was work on your upper back posture.

Be aware of your technique (especially spinal curves) when training and optimise your core strength.

NEUTRAL/STRAIGHT SPINE

A neutral or straight spine is one with Optimal Spinal Curvatures

Thoracic Spine (upper back) 30-35 degrees
Lumbar Spine (lower back) 30-35 degrees
(So technically the spine should never be 'straight', although this term is just used sometimes for simplicity.)

REPETITION RESERVE (RR)

Having a repetition reserve is a great tool for preserving technique in weight training. It basically means you keep a number of reps in reserve, i.e. you could complete a couple more reps (usually one or two) but you don't. This ensures your last rep will be perfect. You achieve the most adaptation on the last rep because that will be the hardest (due to fatigue from the preceding reps).

TEMPO

Tempo is the speed of the exercise in seconds split into parts, e.g. a tempo of '112' on a cable pull means a one-second pull (concentric), a one-second hold at the end range of the movement and a two-second return to the starting point (eccentric). Tempo helps keep the technique and also shows how powerful (speed + strength) a part of the movement should be.

PLYOMETRICS

Plyometrics, also known as jump training, is a training technique designed to increase muscular power and explosiveness.

Plyometric training conditions the body with dynamic resistance exercises that rapidly stretch a muscle (eccentric phase) and then rapidly shorten it (concentric phase). Hopping and jumping exercises, for example, subject the quadriceps to a stretch-shortening cycle that can strengthen these muscles, increase vertical jump, and reduce the force of impact on the joints.

Because plyometric exercises mimic the motions used in sports such as skiing, tennis, football, basketball, volleyball, and boxing, plyometric training often is used to condition professional and amateur adult athletes. But children and adolescents also can benefit from a properly designed and supervised plyometric routine, according to the American College of Sports Medicine.

Plyometric training is associated with many benefits. First popularised in the 1970s by state sports trainers in the former East Germany, it's based on scientific evidence showing that the stretch-shortening cycle prompts the stretch or 'myotactic' reflex of muscle and improves the power of muscular contraction.

But, plyometric training is also associated with some risks, including an increased risk of injury, especially in participants who don't have adequate strength to begin with. So if you're considering plyometrics, it's important to consult with a sports medicine doctor or therapist who can assess your suitability for a plyometrics training programme, and then select a qualified coach or trainer who can gradually introduce you to more difficult exercises.

Source: WebMD

CROSS-TRAINING / VARIETY / FUN

The pain teacher is good but the fun teacher is better!

Too much pain-teacher (see later) and not enough fun make for a dull skier. Yes, you have to put in some effort, but the training can be as fun as the skiing if you get it right.

The 'means' should always align with the 'end' result.

The SAID Principle, discussed before, indicates that to train for skiing you should try and replicate the skiing movements as closely as possible. Well yes and no. Yes, you should try but it will never be totally the same.

YOU CAN NEVER TOTALLY REPLICATE THE SKI ACTIVITY

Even by doing the activity itself because, there are too many variables in skiing:

- weather and snow conditions are always different
- work:rest ratios will always be different on the mountain
- it might be your 1st day skiing or the 6th in a row
- you might have celebrated a 'blue sky powder day' with half a shandy the night before

TRAIN HARD, SKI EASY

It's better to train harder than the activity itself – then you will have extra energy for enjoyment.

Pre-hab, Re-hab and Strength Training

A key concept of training, rather than just doing the activity, is to make yourself better at the activity. To do this you sometimes have to break down the component parts and work on those individually before putting them back together. For example, to make yourself stronger you can perform a barbell front squat, strengthening a key movement pattern of skiing which would not be possible actually skiing.

FUN THEORY

If it's not fun you're not doing it right!

Engaging and Sustainable

Guess what? If it is fun, you might put more into it, try harder and engage the whole body and mind. If it is fun you might even repeat the training programme more than once or twice!

ALL GAIN, NO PAIN

Exercise should not be painful. If it's painful it is not fun. If you are not enjoying your programme, change it. If you are in pain, check your technique, your core strength, your motivation. Are you in the right phase? Have you bitten off more than you can chew? Above all, be nice to yourself!

No pain, no gain' went out with the Dark Ages, however, people are still training by punishing their body for some supposed wrong-doing. Are you training because you dislike yourself or because you love yourself and love skiing? The latter works much better, is more sustainable and is more fun!

VARIETY

Variety is fun and good for the muscles. I work really hard to inject play into my clients' and my own training. This means that we will be ready for anything the mountain or life throws at us. This is especially the case when you get onto the harder, later phases of the programmes such as plyometrics, but of course, variety will also be part of your Phase One 'Exercise Opportunist' stage.

I rarely do the exactly same programme twice. Changes may only be small and do not upset the rhythm and rest times of the programme. For example, once I have completed a couple of sessions of some straight box jumps (Phase 6), I add variety by using a box, BOSU, bench or anything else that allows for endless and spontaneous variations of jumping (forwards, backwards, sideways). With the tractor tyres outside, I always choose a different way of jumping with each set – forwards, sideways, one leg, backwards, on-top/inside, vary position, one tyre ...

You can do the same. Be creative, be spontaneous, have fun!

VARIETY IS NOT JUST FOR THE BODY

Science is starting to show that exercise is more important for the mind:

> ***"There is a direct biological connection between movement and cognitive function... Exercise is the single most powerful tool you have to optimise your brain function."** – John Ratey*
>
> ***The means justify the end.***

NEUROPLASTICITY

Discoveries in modern neuroscience over the last 20 years have generated exciting new ideas for preserving and extending this precious resource. Throughout most of the 20th century, scientists believed that the human nervous system was fundamentally static. No new nerve cells could be generated and in turn, learning and potential were limited. This belief led many to focus on inborn and innate talent, while ignoring the vast potential for training and education.

Today we now know that the human nervous system is incredibly dynamic and is constantly re-sculpting itself in response to lived experience. Not only do we generate new brain cells – a process called neurogenesis – we also modify connections between cells and the insulation around nerve fibres. Collectively, these changes are referred to as neuroplasticity.

The discovery of neuroplasticity tells us that individuals are capable of outrageous growth in almost any skill or capability. By setting up proper environments and conditions, we can facilitate progressive learning throughout a lifespan.

Source: Stresscraft by Frank Forencich www.exuberantanimal.com

BAREFOOT TRAINING

Even though your feet are in rigid ski boots when you are skiing, your feet do a surprising amount of work. Strong, supple, intuitive feet are an essential part of high-performance skiing. Cushion your feet in foam (i.e. normal trainers) when you are training and you will 'dull the senses' and train your feet to be weaker than your body.

The bane of a skier's life is boot pain. If your feet are comfy in the shop but painful after a few hours on the slope, it is most likely a deconditioned foot that is your problem, not the boot.

It may seem counter-intuitive, but exercising/moving (including running) barefoot is more efficient and puts less impact through the body than wearing shoes or trainers.

Barefoot exercise brings the following benefits:

- strengthens intrinsic foot musculature
- maximises biomechanical performance
- enhances proprioception (perception of your body)
- optimises balance and prevents falls
- enhances running efficiency
- facilitates venous return resulting in decreased blood pressure
- decreases ankle sprains
- lowers risk of shin splints
- minimises back pain
- diminishes risk of bunions

Source: Matthew Wallden (www.primalifestyle.com)

Footwear recommended when training is (in order of preference)

Barefoot
Vibram Fivefingers
Minimalist shoes (zero heel drop) such as Vivo Barefoot
Cheap flimsy plimsoles/trainers

STABILITY BALL SIZE

55cm suits most people for the exercises in this programme. Most shops recommend a bigger ball for men but it is not necessary. If you're very tall you might want a 65cm, however, all sizes will work for the exercises in this programme.

CORE STRENGTH

If you haven't heard this training buzzword, where have you been! It might be a buzzword but it is also essential for everything you do. All training should start from the core. Your core is your tummy, back and bottom.

CORE MUSCLES

External Oblique – twist forward
Internal Oblique – twist back. A balance between the two oblique muscles is very important.
Rectus Abdominis – 'the 6 pack' – bends trunk forward. Too many sit-ups shorten these muscles causing postural, respiratory, back and neck problems!
Transversus Abdominis – stabilises lower back and helps extension, i.e. lifting an object from the floor.
Psoas – flexes and stabilises the trunk or hip.
Quadratus Lumborum – must balance with the Psoas for stability and movement.
Gluteus Maximus – your bottom, the key stabiliser and powerhouse for strength and explosive movements.

As always, it is very important to train the core muscles in balance with each other. Many people create imbalances in the core by doing sit-ups/ crunches. Sit-ups are not a functional movement pattern for everyday movement nor skiing, and should only be used sparingly.

Sit-ups create imbalances and hurt your back

INNER AND OUTER CORE

Your inner core muscles are the small but plentiful muscles deep in your core that act as stabilisers. They are the 'marathon runners' that can stabilise all day. Your outer core muscles are the big strong muscles that are needed for strong dynamic movements. They are the sprinters that tire quickly. The problem is that many people are outer core dominant and tire quickly, comprising the stability of the core.

The best core exercises are total body functional exercises or 'integrated' exercises. However, you cannot do them properly if your core is not functioning properly in the first place. Therefore, exercises such as the Lower Abdominal series, in this programme, isolate the inner core muscles to activate and strengthen them so they are active when you come to integrate in the functional movement patterns (see below).

Isolate then integrate.

CHAPTER 4

ISOLATION AND INTEGRATION

Rehab is boring, prehab is fun!

Isolation exercise is pre-habilitation (pre-hab) and re-habilitation (re-hab) exercise. Integration or functional training exercise is high performance training.

Isolation Exercise is training your muscles individually and is good for pre-hab and re-hab but needs to be progressed to integration exercises for high performance. For example, the Lower Abdominal (LA1-4) exercise series in this programme are deigned to isolate, activate and strengthen the inner unit of the lower abdominal muscles. It is really important these muscles are activated as they are the key stabilisers and core support for pretty much every major movement pattern you undertake in sport and everyday life (i.e. functional). Once this is completed, these muscles need to be integrated into the major 'integrated' movement patterns of squat, lunge, bend, push, pull, twist and gait.

Re-habilitation is treatment for injury that has occurred.

Pre-habilitation is to train in such a way that you do not get injured.

Pre-hab is the best, most fun and least expensive option! If you get it right you never need re-hab. If you are injured, you are not fit. If you have to spend 6 weeks on the sidelines, you will be de-conditioning (losing fitness) at a rapid rate. Injury is generally a sign that your training programme is not quite right and the time off is actually an opportunity to improve your training programme (this is the pain teacher). Most injuries are caused by poor training programme and/or training techniques. All great training programmes are pre-habilitation.

Never use fixed weight resistance machines so common in gyms:

- They are not functional (i.e., will not help your body 'function' better in everyday life or sport).
- They make your periphery (arms and legs) stronger and so make your core relatively weaker – not a good plan!
- They also only work a joint at one angle when joints should always move at a slightly different angle.
- They are a throwback from the bodybuilding era where muscles were worked in isolation to look bigger but not to function in any sporting or daily movement pattern.
- 'One size fits all' often will not fit you.

As mentioned throughout this book, you get what you train for. Your muscles are designed, through 4 million years of evolution, to work together and move in 'movement patterns'.

There are seven movement patterns for training which can be made easier, (descended), harder (ascended) or combined to replicate all the movement patterns in sport and everyday living

SEVEN INTEGRATED/FUNCTIONAL MOVEMENT PATTERNS

1. Squat
2. Deadlift
3. Lunge
4. Twist
5. Push
6. Pull
7. Gait (walk/run)

If you cannot perform any of these movement patterns correctly, you can 'descend' the difficulty of the movement pattern to isolate individual muscles and then build them back up (activate and strengthen) to normal standard and then 'ascend' beyond. That's exactly what this programme does.

PROGRESSION EXAMPLE

Squat (1 of 7 Functional Movement Patterns)

Ascending difficulty:

Regression

- Leg press machine – don't bother!
- SB hip raise
- SB wall squat
- Chair squat
- Body weight squat

Basic Human Standard

Progression

- BOSU squat
- DB squat
- DB squat press
- Assisted single leg squat
- Single leg squat on floor (weighted)
- Single leg squat bench
- BB back squat
- BB front squat
- BB overhead squat
- Single leg squat cable pull
- Single leg squat cable press
- BOSU jump
- Lateral hops
- Box jump/tractor tyre
- Coolboard squat
- SB squat
- Single leg jumps onto steps, logs, stones etc
- Slacklining

Skier Minimum Ideal

3 PLANES OF MOTION

1. Saggital - forward and back (the most common)
2. Transverse - twist
3. Frontal – side-to-side (the least common)

Each session should have most if not all functional movement patterns and the three planes of motion.

C) RECOVERY & SUPERCOMPENSATION

The quicker you recover, the more you can train and the better your performance.

You need your parasympathetic nervous system balanced with your sympathetic nervous system: yin with your yang, rest/repair with your fight/flight...

Enhance Recovery/Speed-up Repair:

- Eat better
- Sleep longer and better
- Recovery programme
- Tai Chi
- Better technique when exercising
- Periodisation
- Cold water therapy
- Water
- Pain-teacher

EAT BETTER – FUEL YOUR RECOVERY

Do you know how many calories you burn a day when skiing?

The average is 3000 calories per day – but who's average? I know I can use 5000 calories on a day's skiing. Do not think of calories in terms of weight loss, think of calories in terms of performance. Calories make little difference to weight loss anyway (see below), but in terms of performance (i.e. enjoyment, injury free, not being knackered, etc.) if you are burning 5000 calories a day but only taking in 2,500, how long do you think you can keep this up for?

Time and time again I see people on ski trips not fuelling properly throughout the day and then wondering why they are tired by mid-afternoon. Is it their fitness? Or is it because they only ate 500 calories at breakfast, 800 calories at lunch and have used 3000 calories already that day and still have a 2000 calorie deficit from each of the preceding days?

SUGAR AND THE FIRE

Sugar is energy, but it is also false energy. If you eat food that is very high in sugar (i.e. it releases energy quickly), it is like putting touch-paper on a fire: you get a quick flare up of heat/energy, but this causes the fire to die down cooler than it was before. This is why I would recommend against eating sweets, energy gels, drinks, or any other processed 'crap' – except in emergencies.

You would be better putting 'coal on the fire' for sustainable energy over a longer period of time. However, you cannot put coal on a fire once it has died down or nearly gone out. You have to put coal on the fire proactively, before the heat starts to reduce, and you have to do exactly the same with your body's fuel. You might need a little touch-paper i.e., a quick release of energy (sugary carbohydrates) to occasionally help start a fire if you have let it die down. However, generally you need a mix of slow energy-releasing carbohydrates, high quality proteins and high quality fats. The ratio of each of these macro-nutrients depends on your unique needs which you need to find out for yourself. For more information, see my book *Uncommon Sense: A Practical Guide For Health, Weight Loss & Vitality.*

'One man's food is another man's poison.'
– Lucretius

HIGH QUALITY FAT & PROTEIN

Choose your source very carefully

- Eat non-commercially raised animal fat and protein – grass fed, free range, organic, biodynamic, happy animals… you get the picture. Intensively-raised animal fat can be toxic and damaging to your health. Contrary to popular belief, saturated fat does not cause heart disease or make you fat! Eat cheaper, fattier cuts of meat, eat the skin, gravies, stocks etc, often.
- In addition to meat: avocados, olive oil, butter, coconut oil, eggs.
- Nuts are okay, but don't overdo them and certainly don't eat them everyday. Ideally soak them overnight to remove phytic acid.
- Beware of polyunsaturated fatty acids: baked goods, processed fat, margarines, because if it should be liquid at room temperature and it isn't, avoid it).
- As a rule of thumb, spend more and eat less. Think in terms of buying nutrient density not the size of the portion. This often means you spend less and eat better, especially if you use the bones for stock (see below).

7 Day Sample Food Plan (first featured in Trail Running magazine)							
	MONDAY	**TUESDAY**	**WEDNESDAY**	**THURSDAY**	**FRIDAY**	**SATURDAY**	**SUNDAY**
BREAKFAST	Vegetable juice, cheese omelette, baked quinoa with butter	Buffalo burger, steamed kale, shallots butter	Pinepple, walnuts, cottage cheese, toast, coconut butter	Porridge with goats milk, apple, almonds, boiled egg	Smoothie – coconut oil, yoghurt, mixed berries, chia seeds, banana, apple juice	Bacon, brie, Ryvita, fruit	Smoothie – frozen berries, raw egg, yoghurt, banana, kiwi, applw juice, water
LUNCH	Baked salmon, steamed courgette, steamed wild rice with ghee	Red snapper, steamed asparagus, sliced avocado, olive oil, lemon & herb dressing	Chicken & rice (last night leftovers)	Chilli con carne, cheese salad	Pea, ham, cheese, turnip & celery soup	Wild salmon, lentils, fried courgette, olive oil	Roast beef, gravy, potatoes, greens, braised cabbage
DID YOU KNOW? Coconut oil is a healthy saturated fat, stable at high temperatures so great for cooking but also brilliant raw in smoothies. Olive oil is a monounsaturated fat which is also great for low to medium heat cooking or dressings.							
SNACK	Goats cheese, Ryvita, raw carrot sticks	Pâté, butter, oatcakes	Cheese & raw celery, peppers and cucumber	Nut butter & apple	Smoothie (maybe leftover from breakfast)	Oatcake, butter, sheep's cheese such as Manchego	Flapjack, nuts
DINNER	Roast lamb, basmati rice, salad with olive oil & vinegar	Roast chicken steamed asparagus, greens, wild rice & butter	Baked cod, steamed cauliflower, greens carrots, potato, butter	Grilled pork chops, wild rice, steamed cabbage, butter, tomato & onion salad	Turkey, steamed grean beans, spinach, sweet potato, butter	Chicken stir fry, mixed vegatables, coconut oil	Veg soup, leftover beef, ricecake, butter

THE BEST SPORTS DRINK IN THE WORLD

CHICKEN STOCK/BROTH

Builds powerful ligaments, tendons, and cartilage.

Simmer your chicken carcass for 6-24 hours with cold filtered water, celery, onion, carrot, sea salt, peppercorns, parsley, garlic, vinegar.

Strain the stock and refrigerate it. Once the fat has risen to the top, skim this off as it will contain the most toxins.

The broth keeps for about 5 days in the fridge or freeze it as required.

'The gelatin (in chicken broth) feeds, repairs and calms the mucous lining of the small intestine. It heals the nerves, improves digestion, reduces allergies, relaxes and gives strength.'

– *Sally Fallon, Nourishing Traditions*

SLOW-RELEASE ENERGY CARBOHYDRATES

Carbohydrates include vegetables, fruit, beans and grains. Again, go for quality in terms of nutrient density. Buying organic is the best option, unless you can grow your own.

Slow release – Eat as much as possible: above ground vegetables e.g. greens, beans, peas.

Medium Release – Eat some : below ground vegetables such as potatoes and beetroot, and fruit.

Quick release – Eat as little as possible: grains, bread, rice, pasta.

Be careful with fruit: it contains key vitamins and minerals, but fruit is fructose, the 'ose' meaning sugar. It's 'good' sugar but is still very quick releasing. Try mixing fruit with protein and fat to slow the release of energy down.

You might have heard of the Glycemic Index (GI). It basically relates to how quickly a carbohydrate releases its energy. Low GI is slow releasing; high GI is fast releasing. Also, think in terms of glycemic load, which combines the values of all the foods eaten in a meal remembering that protein and fat will slow down the release of energy. So always eat protein, fat and carbohydrate at every meal and every snack.

NB: If fat and protein were included on the Glycemic Index it would be off the scale, as they release their energy so much slower than carbs. So fat and protein are very beneficial for sustained optimal energy.

WATER

You are 75% water

Most people are dehydrated and toxic due to sugary drinks, caffeine (which actually takes away more water than it gives, a diuretic), dehydrated foods and not actually drinking water.

The first and most important advice I can give an individual looking to increase their performance is to hydrate yourself. This will make you feel better, improve your bodily functions and flush through toxins. Drink filtered water when possible.

HOW MUCH WATER TO DRINK A DAY:

Amount of water in litres per day = your bodyweight in kgs x 0.033

Drink more if you drink water in the form of coffee or tea and even more if it's hot and/or you are sweating a lot.

However, over-hydration — or drinking too much water — is a potentially deadly condition; one that can throw off the balance between water and sodium in your blood. When too much water collects in the body, it can lead to water intoxication or dangerously low levels of sodium in the blood (hyponatremia).

When undertaking a major event such as a big day's skiing or ski touring, be careful to take in minerals as well. If you are eating proactively this will not be a problem. I also recommend a pinch of sea salt in your water bottle (see 'power water' below). I am not a fan of sports drinks because they are just full of toxins and sugar.

POWER WATER

Take a 750ml bottle of water; pour off 100ml. To the remaining 650ml add 4 teaspoons (25g) of dextrose, plus 1/8 (1g) teaspoon of sea salt, plus 1/32 (0.2g) teaspoon of di-potassium phosphate.

This is called 'Power Water'. An athlete can drink this throughout the longest and most demanding athletic competition without the need to drink additional water to maintain hydration, and with confidence that electrolytes are being replaced in perfect proportion.

Buy a 6 or 8 pack of 750ml bottled water and within just a few minutes you can make 6 or 8 bottles of Power Water. You can buy di-potassium phosphate on the internet and the dextrose (glucose) can be found in most healthfood stores.

Source: CHEK Institute

WEIGHT LOSS

If your tummy is over 100cm your health is at serious risk, and more importantly your skiing will improve if you reduce it! Most people do not achieve long-term weight loss when they go on a diet. In fact most people within two years have put more back on than when they started.

Reducing calorie intake will only make you lose muscles tone and not percentage body fat. It will also change the profile in your cells to burn less fat and store more fat. When you return back to your usual eating patterns – which is highly likely, you will have less muscle to burn fat, less cells to burn fat and more cells to store fat. You will get fatter in the long run if you cut calories and this is what all the recent and not so recent scientific research proves.

To lose percentage body fat, focus on what actually works – which is to 'get healthy to lose weight' and not the other way round. A health focus includes the five key elements of nutrition: movement, rest/repair, toxins and mindset. Only a correct approach in all of these five areas will result in sustained weight loss.

If you try and force your body to lose weight, you will have some superficial early success (mostly dehydration and muscle loss) but this leads to a 'bounce back' on increased body fat in the long run. Believe me, it's all documented in research and I've seen it in the flesh with 20 years of personal training. In fact, too much exercise and too little food will increase your percentage body fat. So, to repeat, you have to get healthy to lose weight and not the other way round.

In my view one of the best ways to get healthy is to get ski fit. This is because the best way to lose percentage body fat is to increase muscle.

For more detailed information on weight loss see my book *Uncommon Sense: A Practical Guide to Health, Weight Loss & Vitality* available on Amazon.

SLEEP LONGER AND BETTER

You get stronger when you sleep

Optimally, you should be awake for about 16 hours of the day and asleep for 8 hours of the night. This is hard-wired into our bodies through four million years of evolution. People's sleep patterns are changing through a reduction in the amount of sleep we get and also when we sleep. Only in the last 100 years – a blink of the eye in terms of evolution – has electricity entered our lives and created daylight 24/7. In the same time, lifestyle diseases such as cancer, heart disease, obesity, diabetes etc., have appeared and risen exponentially. Reduce your sleep quantity and quality at your peril.

You receive physical repair in the first four hours of sleep and psychological repair in the second four hours of sleep.

CIRCADIAN RHYTHM

The circadian rhythm is your sleep/wake cycle. Your cortisol (adrenalin) – your 'get-up-and-go' hormone – is highest in the morning through to the early afternoon. As your cortisol levels drop your melatonin, your sleep hormone, starts to build up, rising throughout the evening. Ideally your melatonin level does not drop until the morning giving you deep, restful sleep. If you stimulate your body in the late afternoon and evening you will keep cortisol levels up, suppressing melatonin and therefore reducing the length and quality of your sleep.

An understanding of your circadian rhythm will help you plan your training and recovery.

Aim to:

- Train before 4pm (ideally in the morning)
- Get to sleep before 10:30pm
- Remove all stimulants from the bedroom, e.g TV, phones, computers.

Other sleep tips:

- Avoid stimulation after 9pm e.g. any screens (TV, tablets, phones, computers, etc.) due to stimulating or stressful content, electro-magnetic radiation and flickering light.
- Avoid stimulants in the evening such as sugar, alcohol, caffeine.
- Do your recovery/stretching/breathing programme in the evening.
- Take a hot bath in the evening with Epsom Salts.
- Use blackout blinds for complete darkness.
- Sleep on an 'earthing sheet'.
- Establish a routine: go to bed and get up at the same time everyday.
- Use a sun alarm clock rather than a buzzer.
- Read something uplifting (not stimulating): relaxation CD's and/or journaling all help.

Lack of sleep can:

- weaken immune system
- accelerate tumour growth
- cause weight problems
- impair memory
- decrease physical and mental performance

RECOVERY PROGRAMME

The Recovery Circuit is a key part of your programme but will be overlooked by most people. However, as said above, exercise is all about stimulating recovery and the subsequent supercompensation that goes with it. To achieve high dynamic performance you need to balance it with a bit of the opposite - slow moving, deeply breathing, mindful recovery. This will take your performance to the next level.

TAI CHI CHUAN

My favourite recovery exercise for my body and mind is Tai Chi Chuan. It involves non-stressful movement, meditation and energy centralising, building and circulating. You can also try yoga and mindfulness meditation as well as the above Recovery Circuit. Practise daily.

Find a class at www.taichifinder.co.uk and www.masterdingacademy.com

BETTER TECHNIQUE AND PERIODISATION

As discussed above, technique is the most important aspect of exercising. From a recovery point of view, the better the technique, the less damage you will do and so the quicker you will recover. Likewise, a proper periodised programme gives an opportunity for all the body parts and systems to catch up and recover, e.g. the nervous system, ligaments, tendons as well as muscles.

COLD WATER THERAPY

Cold water therapy includes cold swims, cold showers and cold baths. The cold water works by lowering the damaged tissue's temperature and locally constricting blood vessels. Using cold therapy immediately after an injury helps prevent bruising and swelling from the waste and fluid build-up. Cold also helps numb nerve endings, providing you with instant, localised pain relief.

Ideally, it is best to use cold treatments for the first 48 to 72 hours after exercise or an injury. Water temperature of 10-15 °C (50-59 °F), for about 20-25 minutes is best.
There's always snow and ice when you are skiing, of course. However, you want to take great care in protecting your skin from the intense cold. Always use a cloth or towel wrap. A bag of frozen peas can come in very handy for this purpose. You can apply the ice for 20 minutes, then remove for 20 minutes as this will minimize any potential damage. Start early and repeat as often as you can.

THE PAIN TEACHER

In my training with Paul Chek, he highlights how pain is a powerful teacher; if you don't listen, the Pain Teacher simply keeps giving you *more of what you are creating*, the Pain Teacher amplifies *awareness*. In my own experience, the pain teacher is one of the best teachers I've met. Do not mess around, daydream, or skip her classes or you'll never reach your full potential, resulting in, 'Could do better' reports all round!

Even worse is to do what most people do, and ignore the pain teacher by taking 'treatments' to muffle her. Treatments are generally painkillers in drug format, but can also be any treatment including the complementary ones. Killing the pain teacher is akin to taking out the bulb on a warning light on your car. It gets rid of the symptom but does nothing for the cause nor for your long-term performance (and health).

"Do you take medical drugs? If the answer is yes, what have you avoided or ignored that led to a weakening of your 'self' to the point of needing/wanting medical drugs? Allowing your life to become too stressful is the primary reason for all medical drug consumption and lost time from work!" *– Paul Chek*

ANTI-INFLAMMATORIES

Non-steroidal anti-inflammatory drugs (NSAIDs) work by interfering with particular enzyme systems in the body. They are so commonly taken I've heard them referred to as "Vitamin i" (as in ibuprofen).

Okay, so you take NSAIDs while you're skiing to manage a bit of back pain so that you can enhance your enjoyment of your passion. However, by doing this you are weakening the rest of your body. What happens when your knee is coming under intense pressure? How will you know if you are masking the pain with NSAIDs? The NSAIDs are doing a great job 'muffling' the pain signals, but this means you don't know when to adapt your behaviour (such as changing muscles recruitment), therefore, your knee receives none of the 'help' it is asking for and will 'breakdown' forcing you into an abrupt change of behaviour, often involving helicopters and a mad panic to check your insurance cover – i.e. injury! This then leads you to intensive physiotherapy for the knee, but this it not getting to the root cause. At a guess, the root cause was poor core strength leading to back pain, leading to anti-inflammatories, leading to pain signal 'muffling', leading to unsupported knee, leading to shortened ski fun!

Listen to your body constantly and adapt your training and your behaviour accordingly. Any attempt to 'muffle' pain for any length of time is a wasted opportunity for enhanced performance.

NSAIDS SIDE EFFECTS

Common side effects include:

- Indigestion
- Stomach ulcers - a sore in the lining of the stomach, gastrointestinal perforation – where a hole occurs in the wall of your stomach or intestines causing gastrointestinal bleeding – internal bleeding within the digestive system
- Anaemia – where blood is unable to carry enough oxygen around your body which can cause shortness of breath and tiredness
- Increased blood pressure

Less common side effects include headaches, feeling drowsy or dizzy.

Rarely NSAIDs can affect your heart and the rest of the circulatory system causing heart failure – where the heart is having trouble pumping enough blood around the body, potentially resulting in heart attack, hypertension (high blood pressure that needs treatment) or stroke.

Source: NHS Website

GLOSSARY

BB .... Barbell
BOSU .... Acronym for 'Both Sides Up' an inflatable dome shaped balance challenge aid.
BW .... Bodyweight i.e. no extra weights
DB .... Dumbbell
Isometric............ Strength work without any movement
MB............ Medicine Ball
Plyos .... Plyometrics (rebounding movements like jumping)
Prone .... Face/front downwards
Reps .... Repetitions of each exercise
RM............ Repetition Maximum (the maximum weight you can lift, eg. 1RM is the maximum lift you can lift once)
RR .... Repetition reserve - a number of repetitions you could complete but you do not complete to ensure optimum technique.
SB .... Stability Ball (also means Swiss Ball)
Secs .... Seconds
Sets .... A number of repetitions is a set
Supine .... Face/front upwards
Tech. .... Focus on precise technique rather than number or difficulty
Tempo .... Speed of exercise in seconds, with an option to split into parts eg. 1-2-1 (see Chapter 4)
↘ .... The green shading linking exercises and arrow in rest section is a 'Superset' which means you go straight on to the linked exercise without rest and then, if completing another set, rest the stated time, and then go back to the first exercise (like a mini-circuit)
TRX .... Brand name for a suspension strap, often used for pulling exercises.

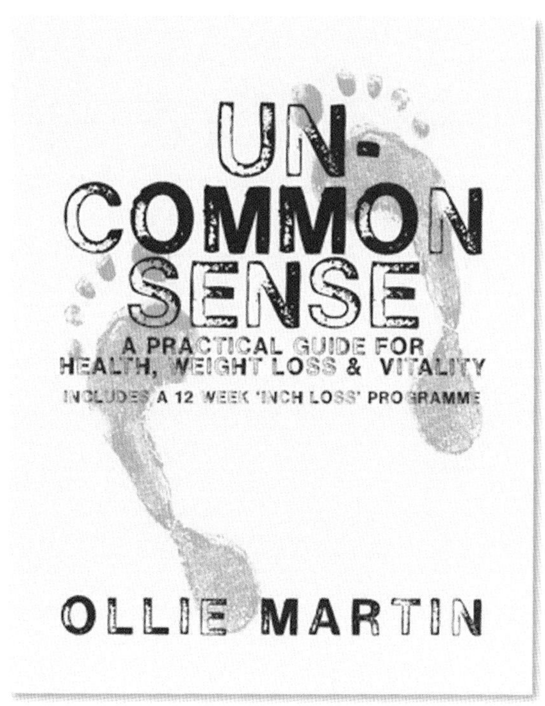

"Ollie Martin has done the world a great favour by distilling health and wellness down into those key topics and bits of information that should be 'common sense', but sadly, are not today. Those wanting a straight-forward book to guide them into living well will be pleased with this simple, easy to apply book written by a truly skilled CHEK Institute-trained Holistic Lifestyle Coach, and excellent athlete."

Paul Chek

Founder of the CHEK Institute, and internationally renowned health expert

Printed in Great Britain
by Amazon

81348008R00074